THE ECONOMICS
OF MINORITIES

ECONOMICS INFORMATION GUIDE SERIES

Series Editor: Robert W. Haseltine, Associate Professor of Economics,
State University College of Arts and Science at Geneseo, Geneseo, New York

Also in this series:

CONSUMER EDUCATION—*Edited by Terry A. Darveaux**

HISTORY OF ECONOMIC ANALYSIS—*Edited by William K. Hutchinson**

RUSSIAN ECONOMIC HISTORY—*Edited by Daniel and Vera Kazmer**

TRANSPORTATION ECONOMICS—*Edited by James P. Rakowski**

ECONOMIC EDUCATION—*Edited by Catherine Hughes**

HEALTH AND MEDICAL ECONOMICS—*Edited by Ted J. Ackroyd**

LABOR ECONOMICS—*Edited by Ross E. Azevedo**

ECONOMIC HISTORY OF CANADA—*Edited by Trevor J. O. Dick**

MATHEMATICAL ECONOMICS AND OPERATIONS RESEARCH—
Edited by Joseph Zaremba*

MONEY, BANKING, AND MACROECONOMICS—*Edited by James M. Rock**

INTERNATIONAL TRADE—*Edited by Ahmed M. El-Dersh***

ECONOMIC DEVELOPMENT—*Edited by Thomas A. Bieler***

*in press
**in preparation

The above series is part of the
GALE INFORMATION GUIDE LIBRARY

The Library consists of a number of separate series of guides covering
major areas in the social sciences, humanities, and current affairs.

General Editor: Paul Wasserman, Professor and former Dean, School of
Library and Information Services, University of Maryland

THE ECONOMICS OF MINORITIES

A GUIDE TO INFORMATION SOURCES

Volume 2 in the Economics Information Guide Series

Kenneth L. Gagala

Assistant Professor, New York State School of Industrial and Labor Relations, Cornell University

Gale Research Company

Book Tower, Detroit, Michigan 48226

**Library of Congress
Cataloging in Publication Data**

Gagala, Kenneth L.
   The economics of minorities.

   (Economics information guide series; v. 2)
(Gale information guide library)
     1. Negroes--Economic conditions--Bibliography.
2. Indians of North America--Economic conditions--
Bibliography.   3. Spanish Americans in the United
States--Economic conditions--Bibliography.   I. Title.
Z1361.N39G26 [E185.8]   330.9'73   73-17573
ISBN 0-8103-1294-8

VITA

Kenneth L. Gagala received the Ph.D. in Economics from Michigan State University in 1970. He has published articles in the AMERICAN ECONOMIST, JOURNAL OF BLACK STUDIES, SOCIAL SCIENCE RECORD, JOURNAL OF SOCIAL STUDIES, and others. He is an assistant professor at the New York State School of Industrial and Labor Relations, Cornell University, and serves as statewide coordinator for Cornell's Labor Studies Program.

CONTENTS

PREFACE

This volume organizes and briefly summarizes research on the economic conditions of nonwhite people in the United States. Nonwhites comprise approximately 12 percent of the population. In this volume, unlike the Bureau of Census definition, American Indians, blacks, Mexican-Americans, and Puerto Ricans are viewed as nonwhite.

Blacks comprise about 95 percent of the nonwhite population. Likewise, approximately that proportion of the material in this volume is concerned with black Americans. This concentration reflects the composition of research on nonwhites.

Much of the material in the volume does not come within the purview of what has generally come to be known as modern economics, and might be more properly categorized as political or social economy. There is a good reason. The researcher who comprehends the effects of social and political forces upon minorities lends realism to his analysis in terms of both methodological design and policy recommendations.

Research in other social sciences also provides fertile ground for economic research topics. One may ask, for example, what psychologist Gordon Allport's THE NATURE OF PREJUDICE can provide to the economist. Allport hypothesizes that discrimination resulting from prejudicial attitudes is apt to be more prevalent in employment situations involving interpersonal relations between whites and nonwhites. Subsequently, economists investigating the structural nature of employment discrimination found higher discrimination coefficients in occupational categories involving high rates of white-nonwhite interpersonal relations than occupations with low rates of interpersonal relations.

The bulk of the material cited in this volume was published during the period 1965 to the summer of 1974. Prior to 1965 little research on minorities was conducted. The urban riots of the mid to late 1960s appear to have provided the stimulus for the increase in scholarly inquiry. As the 1970s progressed, the quantity of research declined. Perhaps this is a reflection of a succession of quiet summers.

Preface

In a small number of cases, certain information may be missing in the citations. I came by these references in either one of two ways. I read them while conducting the research on my dissertation, or they were cited in journal advertisements. I believe, however, that this volume benefits from their inclusion.

Kenneth L. Gagala

Chapter 1

DESCRIPTION AND CAUSES
OF BLACK ECONOMIC INEQUALITY

Chapter 1

DESCRIPTION AND CAUSES

OF BLACK ECONOMIC INEQUALITY

Adams, Arvil V[an]. "Black-White Occupational Differentials in Southern Metropolitan Employment." JOURNAL OF HUMAN RESOURCES 7 (Fall 1972): 500-517.

> Adams finds that within twenty-five southern metropolitan areas black women had a more identical occupational distribution with their white counterparts than black men. The relative occupational distribution of black men is largely determined by education and industrial composition differentials. A set of variables over which employers exercise little control--education, age, economic growth, skill requirements, industry composition, and market size--contribute heavily to explaining the black-white relative occupational distribution.

Ashenfelter, Orley. "Changes in Labor Market Discrimination over Time." JOURNAL OF HUMAN RESOURCES 5 (Fall 1970): 403-30. Tables.

> Ashenfelter estimates that changes in the relative earnings of nonwhite workers may be attributed to changes in discrimination in the postwar period, and tests hypotheses about the effect that cyclical swings in aggregate labor market activity may have had on discrimination against black men over the period 1960 to 1966. While a significant reduction in discrimination against black women occurred, cyclical swings in aggregate labor market activity had little effect on the extent of discrimination.

Baron, Harold M., and Hymer, Bennett. "The Negro Worker in the Chicago Labor Market." THE NEGRO AND THE AMERICAN LABOR MOVEMENT, pp. 232-85. Edited by Julius Jacobson. Garden City, N.Y.: Doubleday & Co., 1968.

> Baron and Hymer describe the operation of a dual labor market mechanism in the employment of black workers in Chicago. During periods of peak demand, blacks are utilized to fill shortages in nontraditional black jobs. When demand declines, blacks are the first to be dismissed. The dual labor market mechanism is perpetuated by employer and union discrimination and discriminatory education and housing practices which impede the employability of

black workers.

Batchelder, Alan B. THE ECONOMICS OF POVERTY. New York: John Wiley & Sons, 1966. 214 p. Tables.

Batchelder examines the nature of poverty, its causes, and possible solutions. Poverty is consistent with the operation of a market economy. Transfer programs under government auspices can reduce income inequality, but in the long run, structural changes in the institutions perpetuating poverty are necessary.

_____. "The Economy and the Minority Poor." In THE DISADVANTAGED POOR: EDUCATION AND EMPLOYMENT, pp. 123-52. By Task Force on Economic Growth and Opportunity. Washington, D.C.: 1966.

Batchelder assesses the socioeconomic condition of four racial and ethnic minorities. He attributes much of this disadvantaged condition to poor education and hypothesizes that the return on investment in education will be high because minorities with above average native intelligence are prevented from fulfilling their potential.

Bergmann, Barbara R. "The Effect on White Incomes of Discrimination in Employment." JOURNAL OF POLITICAL ECONOMY 79 (March/April 1971): 294-313. Tables.

Bergmann states that discrimination concentrates blacks into certain occupations while excluding them from others. In the occupations to which blacks are relegated, marginal productivity may be lowered by the enforced abundance of supply. A model with this crowding hypothesis is used to estimate the effects on white incomes by a reduction in discrimination. Whites with an elementary education might lose 10 percent of their income; the effect is miniscule on all other whites and the national income.

Bergmann, Barbara R., and Krause, William R. "Evaluating and Forecasting Progress in Racial Integration of Employment." INDUSTRIAL AND LABOR RELATIONS REVIEW 25 (April 1972): 399-409.

By examining the proportion of blacks comprising new hires and separations, Bergmann and Krause predict the time at which blacks will comprise a representative proportion of various occupational categories. Very slow progress has occurred since 1968, particularly in white-collar occupations. To make significant progress, blacks must be hired in ever increasing proportions for nontraditional occupations.

Bergmann, Barbara R., and Lyle, Jerolyn R. "The Occupational Standing of Negroes by Areas and Industries." JOURNAL OF HUMAN RESOURCES 6 (Fall 1971): 411-33. Tables.

Bergmann and Lyle examine indexes on the occupational standing of blacks relative to whites in major metropolitan areas and industries. Using the percentage voting for Governor Wallace in 1968 as a criterion, they found that the most important factor in explaining differences in the indexes among areas is the citizens' attitudes toward equality for blacks. Although the rate of net in-migration was also important, variables designed to measure differences among areas in the black-white education gap and in the availability of public transportation are inadequate predictors. Blacks have poorer occupational status in industries which are more heavily involved in government contracting. Economic growth of an industry and a relatively small proportion of white-collar jobs in an industry are conconducive to a better occupational distribution for blacks.

Blau, Peter M., and Duncan, Otis Dudley. "Inequality of Opportunity." In THE AMERICAN OCCUPATIONAL STRUCTURE, pp. 207-41. By Peter M. Blau and Otis Dudley Duncan. New York: John Wiley & Sons, 1967. Tables.

Blau and Duncan document the low degree of upward occupational mobility of black men over a period of time.

Blinder, Alan S. "Wage Discrimination: Reduced Form and Structural Estimates." JOURNAL OF HUMAN RESOURCES 8 (Fall 1973): 436-55.

Blinder compiles regression equations explaining the wage rates of white males, black males, and white females to analyze the black-white wage differential among men. Seventy percent of the overall differential income between black and white males is attributable to discrimination.

Bloch, Herman D. "Discrimination against the Negro in Employment in New York, 1920-1963." AMERICAN JOURNAL OF ECONOMICS AND SOCIOLOGY 24 (October 1965): 361-82.

Bloch observes that the mechanisms for keeping blacks in the lowest economic strata are: (1) the complete denial of black employment in an industry or work place; (2) partial restriction of black employment or confinement of blacks to menial, arduous, or dirty jobs; (3) discriminatory retrenchment or the principle of "last to be hired, first to be fired," irrespective of length of service. Bloch documents the existence of these three mechanisms in New York City.

_____. "Some Economic Effects of Discrimination." AMERICAN JOURNAL OF ECONOMICS AND SOCIOLOGY 25 (January 1966): 11-23. Tables.

Bloch finds that restrictions upon job mobility hamper the occupational mobility of blacks. The lack of job and occupational mobility affect the economic security status of blacks. The effect is to reinforce white stereotypes and continue a vicious circle. The cycle of deprivation is a useful analytical device for examining the effects of various policy proposals.

Bloice, Carl. "The Black Worker's Future under American Capitalism." BLACK SCHOLAR 3 (May 1972): 14-22.

Bloice observes that blacks are concentrated in unskilled and semi-skilled jobs in the automotive, steel, and electronics industries. Automation and the transference of operations abroad are particularly difficult for black workers. Bloice concludes that the future of black workers is bleak.

Brazziel, William F. "Black-White Comparability in College Enrollment." JOURNAL OF HUMAN RESOURCES 5 (Winter 1970): 106-16. Tables.

Brazziel reports that black-white comparability in jobs and housing will never be realized until comparability in college enrollments and graduation for blacks is achieved. The education gap between races is widening, while labor force demands for college training are increasing.

Briggs, Vernon M., Jr. NEGRO EMPLOYMENT IN THE SOUTH. Vol. 1: THE HOUSTON LABOR MARKET. Washington, D.C.: U.S. Department of Labor, Manpower Administration, 1971. 103 p. Tables.

Briggs reports that despite expanding labor demand and labor shortages, Houston blacks have experienced little advancement into higher-paying occupations. For black men the major obstacle appears to be a lack of training, for black women, discrimination.

Brown, David L. "Percent Nonwhite and Racial Disparity in Nonmetropolitan Cities in the South." SOCIAL SCIENCE QUARTERLY 53 (December 1972): 573-82.

Brown observes that the white-nonwhite income differential increases in direct proportion to the percentage nonwhites comprise of the nonmetropolitan areas of the South. However, the proportion of non-whites in higher-status occupational categories also increases when the proportion of nonwhites in these areas is greater.

Bullock, Paul. POVERTY IN THE GHETTO AND POVERTY IN LOS ANGELES. Los Angeles: Institute of Industrial Relations, University of California at Los Angeles, 1966. 6 p. Tables.

Bullock provides a statistical description of the black poor in Los Angeles.

Cassell, Frank H. "Chicago 1960-1970: One Small Step Forward." INDUSTRIAL RELATIONS 9 (May 1970): 277-93. Tables.

Little improvement in black employment rates and occupational distribution occurred in Chicago between 1960 and 1970. Toward the end of the decade black political power in the city began a translation into programs which offered the prospect of improving economic conditions. The future of black employment in the city, according to Cassell, cannot be divorced from political process.

Chicago Commission on Race Relations. NEW NEGRO IN CHICAGO. Chicago: University of Chicago Press, 1922. 425 p. Tables.

This investigatory commission report on the 1919 Chicago race riot examines the condition of black housing, education, employment, and public accommodations. De jure segregation is well documented. The report provides interesting parallels when examined along with later riot commission reports.

Chiswick, Barry R. "Racial Discrimination in the Labor Market: A Test of Alternative Hypotheses." JOURNAL OF POLITICAL ECONOMY 81 (November/December 1973): 1330-53. Tables.

If firms do not view white and nonwhite workers as interchangeable, there will be little integration of work forces. Where employers discriminate, white workers of a given skill level will receive higher weekly wages while working with nonwhites. This pattern of discrimination creates a component of income inequality within skill levels. Chiswick tests this hypothesis and finds evidence of discrimination.

Citizens Board of Inquiry into Hunger and Malnutrition in the United States. HUNGER, U.S.A. Boston: Beacon Press, 1968. 96 p.

The report describes the relationship between government agricultural programs and the nutritional needs of the poor. It recommends a vast overhaul of the existing food delivery system.

Clark, Kenneth B. DARK GHETTO: DILEMMAS OF SOCIAL POWER. New York: Harper & Row, Publishers, 1965. 240 p.

Clark examines the conditions of black youth in Harlem and formulates a separate socioeconomic infrastructure for the black minority in a white-dominated society.

Corazzini, Arthur J. "Equality of Employment Opportunity in the Federal White Collar Civil Service." JOURNAL OF HUMAN RESOURCES 7 (Fall 1972): 424-45. Tables.

Corazzini investigates the returns on several measures of worker productivity, and measures the average salary differential between whites and nonwhites, males and females--with these two latter variables held constant. He finds that black males and females earned considerably less than whites with comparable employment characteristics.

Crain, Robert L. "School Integration and Occupational Achievement of Negroes." AMERICAN JOURNAL OF SOCIOLOGY 75 (January 1970): 593-606.

The author compares the occupational attainment of blacks attending segregated schools with that of blacks attending integrated schools. The latter had higher earnings, greater concentration in skilled jobs, and knew more white college graduates, who are potential sources of employment information. Crain concludes that segregation not only affects educational attainment but also employment information.

Detroit Urban League. A PROFILE OF THE DETROIT NEGRO 1959-1964. Detroit: 1965. 35 p. Tables.

> The report describes the housing, education, employment, and income status of blacks in Detroit and examines reasons for these conditions.

Doeringer, Peter B., and Piore, Michael J. "Equal Employment Opportunity in Boston." INDUSTRIAL RELATIONS 9 (May 1970): 324-39.

> In Boston, the progress blacks have achieved in attaining better paying jobs is the result of employers practicing equal opportunity programs, and tight labor market conditions. A decline in general economic conditions, however, can easily eliminate black job gains and future improvement.

_____. INTERNAL LABOR MARKETS AND MANPOWER ANALYSIS. Lexington, Mass.: D. C. Heath & Co., 1971. 214 p. Tables and charts.

> Doeringer and Piore contend that racial discrimination occurs for two reasons: the high cost to employers for screening, recruiting, and training minorities; and attempts by white workers to enhance their job security and wages at the expense of minorities.

Duncan, Otis Dudley. "Inheritance of Poverty or Inheritance of Race?" In ON UNDERSTANDING POVERTY, pp. 85-110. Edited by Daniel P. Moynihan. New York: Basic Books, 1969.

> Duncan contends that poverty among blacks is a result of receiving unequal treatment from society, rather than being born to poor parents--the cause of the "cycle of poverty." If discrimination were eliminated, the high incidence of poverty among blacks would be drastically reduced.

_____. "Patterns of Occupational Mobility among Negro Men." POPULATION INDEX 33 (July-September 1967): 309-10.

> Duncan observes that while white men tend to move into higher paying, higher status occupations than their fathers held, black men do not experience intergenerational upward occupational mobility.

Duncan, Otis Dudley, and Duncan, Beverly. THE NEGRO POPULATION OF CHICAGO. Chicago: University of Chicago Press, 1957. 330 p. Tables.

> The Duncans intensively analyze demographic statistics on the black population of Chicago. The methods of analysis should be of particular interest to the researcher.

Eckstein, Otto. EDUCATION, EMPLOYMENT, AND NEGRO EQUALITY. Washington, D.C.: U.S. Department of Labor, Manpower Administration, 1968. 23 p. Tables.

Eckstein reports that, if present trends continue, black participation
in higher paying occupational categories will increase very slowly.
He recommends a vast increase in the rate at which blacks are included in the educational mainstream.

Fendrich, James M. "The Returning Black Vietnam-Era Veterans." SOCIAL
SERVICE REVIEW 46 (March 1972): 60-75.

Fendrich describes the employment situation confronted by returning
black Vietnam veterans and their attitudes toward social service
institutions.

Flanagan, Robert J. "Segmented Market Theories and Racial Discrimination."
INDUSTRIAL RELATIONS 12 (October 1973): 253-73. Tables.

Flanagan reports that housing segregation does not appear to depress
the economic returns to blacks for their education and work experience. The important barrier to higher black incomes appears to
be access to on-the-job training. Low rates of OJT are attributable
to the poor quality of education blacks receive.

Fogel, Walter. "The Effect of Low Educational Attainment on Incomes: A
Comparative Study of Selected Ethnic Groups." JOURNAL OF HUMAN RE-
SOURCES 1 (Summer 1966): 22-40. Tables.

Fogel reports that a given educational attainment level has less
income value for disadvantaged minority groups than for whites.
While the relative size of a minority group in a local population
is unimportant, the more closely members approach the appearance
of whites, the greater their economic potential. Educational attainment accounts for about half the income differential between
whites and minorities. Quality of education and discrimination
are probably the other determinants.

Formby, John P. "The Extent of Wage and Salary Discrimination Against Non-
White Labor." SOUTHERN ECONOMIC JOURNAL 35 (October 1968): 140-
50.

Formby estimates the extent of wage and salary discrimination based
on the aggregate income differential between whites and nonwhites
in matched age-education categories. According to Formby's cal-
culations, the cost of discrimination adjusted for price changes increased from $4 billion in 1949 to $6.6 billion for 1959, a 20
percent per capita increase.

Franklin, Raymond S. "A Framework for the Analysis of Interurban Negro-
White Economic Differentials." INDUSTRIAL AND LABOR RELATIONS RE-
VIEW 21 (April 1968): 367-74.

Franklin contends that the degree of prejudice against blacks, as
expressed in black-white income and occupational-status differentials, depends upon whether industry is capital intensive or labor

intensive. Unlike the latter, capital intensive industries show less discrimination because interpersonal relations between whites and blacks are less. Attitudes of whites toward middle-class blacks derive from attitudes toward blacks in low income, low status jobs. By changing the occupational distribution of blacks, discrimination would be effectively attacked.

Freeman, Richard B. "Decline of Labor Market Discrimination and Economic Analysis." AMERICAN ECONOMIC REVIEW 63 (May 1973): 280–86. Tables.

Freeman observes that substantial improvements in the position of black workers occurred in the 1960s. Discrimination appears to be more a matter of "economic gain" for the dominant group rather than a matter of "taste." Discrimination by the government is a significant factor. The political position of blacks is an important determinant of economic progress.

Friedman, Milton. CAPITALISM AND FREEDOM. Chicago: University of Chicago Press, 1962. 202 p.

The market mechanism, according to Friedman, is more potent than government action as a force for improving the economic status of nonwhites. Government actions interfere with the market mechanism, and nonwhites would be in a worse economic position if the capitalistic system had not dominated in the United States.

Gagala, Ken. "The Dual Urban Labor Market." JOURNAL OF BLACK STUDIES 3 (March 1973): 350–70.

Gagala develops a two sector model for occupations with low black participation. In the short run, blacks are utilized to fill shortages in the white sector, which is comprised of nontraditional black jobs. The dual urban-labor market model is utilized to examine the effects of antidiscrimination, manpower training, and quota employment policies.

Gallaway, Lowell. "The Foundations of the 'War on Poverty.'" AMERICAN ECONOMIC REVIEW 55 (March 1965): 122–31.

Gallaway observes that economic growth has been the primary reason for a reducation in the incidence of poverty in the United States. Without a high level of sustained economic growth, antipoverty programs sponsored by the federal government will have only a minimal effect.

_____. "The Negro and Poverty." JOURNAL OF BUSINESS 40 (January 1967): 27–35.

Gallaway documents the disproportionate number of blacks comprising the poor. Among the prime reasons cited is the low educational attainment of blacks. Raising the educational level of blacks would substantially reduce poverty.

. "Unemployment Levels Among Nonwhite Teenagers." UNIVERSITY OF CHICAGO JOURNAL OF BUSINESS 42 (July 1969): 265-76. Tables.

Between 1954 and 1966, increasing supply and declining demand caused the unemployment rate of nonwhite male teenagers to rise by 75 percent despite a 20 percent decline in total unemployment. A 4.5 to 5 percent economic growth rate is necessary throughout the 1970s to reattain the 1954 level. According to Galloway, the likelihood of this occurring is small.

Geschwender, James. A. "Negro Education: The False Faith." PHYLON 29 (Winter 1968): 371-79. Tables.

Geschwender examines the hypothesis that improved education alone will improve the economic condition of blacks. Through the an-alysis of time series and cross-section data on income, education, and occupation, he deems the hypothesis false.

Giles, Robert H. "How to Become a Target City." THE REPORTER 36 (June 1967): 38-41.

Giles describes the socioeconomic condition of blacks in Cleveland, Ohio.

Ginzberg, Eli. "Poverty and the Negro. In THE DISADVANTAGED POOR: EDUCATION AND EMPLOYMENT, pp. 207-28. By Task Force on Economic Employment. Washington, D.C.: Chamber of Commerce of the United States, 1966.

Ginzberg provides a vivid description of the impoverished condi-tions under which a large proportion of the black population ex-ists.

Gordon, David M. "Income and Welfare in New York City." THE PUBLIC INTEREST, 16 (Summer 1969): 64-68.

While nonwhites comprise 25 percent of New York City's population, they represent 75 percent of the poor. Family size is directly cor-related with poverty. Gordon observes that a reduction in the incidence of poverty would reduce family size.

Green, Constance McLaughlin. THE SECRET CITY: A HISTORY OF RACE RELATIONS IN THE NATION'S CAPITAL. Princeton, N.J.: Princeton Uni-versity Press, 1967. 389 p.

Green traces the condition of blacks in Washington, D.C., from 1791 to 1961.

Greenleigh Associates, Inc. A STUDY: THOSE NOT WORKING IN A TIGHT LABOR MARKET, MILWAUKEE, WISCONSIN. New York: 1967. 101 p. Tables.

Blacks were among the unemployed studied. Lack of skill and

employer discrimination were identified as major factors contributing to black unemployment despite high demand in the Milwaukee, Wisconsin, labor market.

Guthrie, Harold W. "The Prospect of Equality of Incomes between White and Black Families under Varying Rates of Unemployment." JOURNAL OF HUMAN RESOURCES 5 (Fall 1970): 431-46. Tables.

Guthrie finds that when the unemployment rate is low, growth rates for income are higher among black families than among white families, while in the middle range of the income distribution, rising unemployment is more disadvantageous to black families than to white families. At a stable 3.5 percent unemployment rate, however, equality of incomes could be achieved in about twenty-five years. Guthrie estimates that if unemployment rises to a stable 4.5 percent, income equality would be achieved in fifty years.

Gwartney, James D. "Discrimination, Achievement, and Payoffs of a College Degree." JOURNAL OF HUMAN RESOURCES 7 (Winter 1972): 60-70.

At various levels of educational attainment, blacks score lower than whites on educational achievement tests; comparing average grade level achievement with income shows that the apparent income differential due to discrimination is reduced substantially across sex, age, and regional groupings. The differential is lowest for college graduates. Therefore, in order to equalize black with white incomes, the quality of black education must be upgraded.

_____. "Discrimination and Income Differentials." AMERICAN ECONOMIC REVIEW 60 (June 1970): 396-408.

Gwartney attempts to break down the income differential between whites and nonwhites into two categories--that resulting from differences in productivity factors not directly related to discrimination, and that not accounted for by productivity factors and which may result largely from employment discrimination. Because of the effect of discrimination on education and housing, the two factors are not completely separable.

Gwartney, James D., and Mccaffree, Kenneth M. "Variance in Discrimination among Occupations." SOUTHERN ECONOMIC JOURNAL 38 (October 1971): 141-55. Tables.

Gwartney and Mccaffree report that the intensity of discrimination varies among major occupational groups on the basis of relative income ratios between nonwhites and whites. Sales and managerial occupations, some professions where consumer contact is important, and the construction and metal crafts generally are areas of high discrimination. Among operatives, most clerical and service workers, and occupations somewhat remote from consumer contacts, employment discrimination and low-income ratios are not as easily found.

Harriman, George. "Race Prejudice: The Economic Swindle." AVE MARIA 104 (September 1966): 7-10.

Harriman observes that discrimination in education and employment prevents blacks from realizing their full economic potential. Failure to fully develop human resources lowers the total national income.

Harrison, Bennett. "Education and Underemployment in the Urban Ghetto." AMERICAN ECONOMIC REVIEW 62 (December 1972): 796-812.

Education appears to bear no significant correlation with employment regularity for blacks. Therefore, government policies for increasing black education will not reduce the unemployment problem. Emphasis should be placed on increasing the demand for black labor.

Henderson, George. "Beyond Poverty of Income." JOURNAL OF NEGRO EDUCATION 36 (Winter 1967): 42-50.

Henderson observes that low incomes have a debilitating effect upon much of the black community. Poverty causes sociological and psychological harm, which may be greater than the inability to satisfy economic needs.

Hiestand, Dale L. ECONOMIC GROWTH AND EMPLOYMENT OPPORTUNITIES FOR MINORITIES. New York: Columbia University Press, 1964. 702 p. Tables.

Hiestand examines the effect of economic growth on the occupational and income condition of nonwhites. He concludes that the major factor for improving the economic condition of minorities is noneconomic, such as a reduction in employer discrimination. Expansionary, monetary, and fiscal policies have a minimal effect upon the black economic condition.

_____. "Equal Employment in New York City." INDUSTRIAL RELATIONS 9 (May 1970): 294-307. Tables.

Since 1960, improved employment has occurred in New York City for blacks and Puerto Ricans in white collar occupations. The reasons are a general increase in white-collar employment, training programs, and equal employment programs by government, business, and labor unions.

_____. WHITE COLLAR EMPLOYMENT OPPORTUNITIES FOR MINORITIES IN NEW YORK CITY. Washington, D.C.: U.S. Equal Employment Opportunity Commission. 70 p. Tables. Sold by Government Printing Office.

Hiestand finds blacks and Puerto Ricans concentrated at the lower end of the hierarchical structure of white-collar employment in New York City. Improved educational opportunities for minorities and the dispersal of information on existing employment opportunities throughout minority communities would advance their positions in the white-collar employment structure.

Hilaski, Harvey [J.] "Unutilized Manpower in Poverty Areas of Six Cities." MONTHLY LABOR REVIEW 94 (December 1971): 45-52.

Hilaski reports that the proportion of nonlabor force participants desiring work is significantly higher in poverty areas than in non-poverty areas. More blacks than whites desire work in the six cities surveyed.

Hill, Herbert. "Demographic Change and Racial Ghettos." JOURNAL OF URBAN LAW 44 (Winter 1966): 231-85.

Holland, Susan S. "Adult Men Not in the Labor Force." MONTHLY LABOR REVIEW 90 (March 1967): 5-15. Tables.

Holland compares the labor force participation rates of white and black men.

Jacobs, Paul. "The Lower Depths in Los Angeles." MIDSTREAM 13 (May 1967): 14-23.

According to Jacobs, public and private employment agencies generally neglect unskilled black workers. The lack of economic fulfillment affects attitudes and aspirations toward education and social conduct, making employment opportunities even worse.

Kahn, Tom. THE ECONOMICS OF EQUALITY. New York: League for Industrial Democracy, 1964. 70 p. Tables.

Kahn views the civil rights movement as an instrument for attaining more than minority rights. Only through the achievement of basic structural change, it is argued, will the minority and the majority achieve a solution to basic economic inequality within the American class structure.

Kain, John F., comp. RACE AND POVERTY: THE ECONOMICS OF DISCRIMINATION. Englewood Cliffs, N.J.: Prentice-Hall, 1969. 186 p.

A book of readings that primarily contains articles cited elsewhere in this bibliography.

Kalvans, Irena. "Economic Brief on Conditions of Negroes in the United States and in Detroit." MICHIGAN MANPOWER QUARTERLY REVIEW 4 (Winter 1968): 12-15. Tables.

The socioeconomic condition of blacks residing in Detroit is substantially better than that of blacks residing in other areas of the United States.

Kapel, David E. "Environmental Factors, Student Variables, and Employment

Adjustment of Male Negroes." JOURNAL OF NEGRO EDUCATION 39 (Fall 1970): 333-40.

Kapel correlates the effects of the degree of racial integration in the schools, the type of community in which the school is located, and the region of the country with income received after graduation. The region of the country (North v. South) appears to be the most influential factor determining the income of black men.

Katzman, Martin T. "Discrimination, Subculture, and the Economic Performance of Negroes, Puerto Ricans, and Mexican Americans." AMERICAN JOURNAL OF ECONOMICS AND SOCIOLOGY 27 (October 1968): 371-76. Tables.

Katzman attempts to differentiate the effects of discrimination by employers and unions from the effects of the sociopsychological characteristics of minorities on economic performance. Attitudes toward present versus future gratification, work versus leisure, pecuniary versus nonpecuniary job benefits, and education are important determinants for income differentials between whites and nonwhites. Also, these social-class factors are often the grounds for discrimination by whites.

_____. "Opportunity, Subculture and the Economic Performance of Urban Ethnic Groups." AMERICAN JOURNAL OF ECONOMICS AND SOCIOLOGY 28 (October 1969): 351-66.

Katzman examines the economic status of fourteen ethnic groups in nine metropolitan areas. The performance of ethnic groups varies with the general economic conditions of the cities in which they reside. In all metropolitan areas Katzman studied, educational attainment appears to be a major determinant for their economic condition.

_____. "Urban Racial Minorities and Immigrant Groups: Some Economic Comparisons." AMERICAN JOURNAL OF ECONOMICS AND SOCIOLOGY 30 (January 1971): 15-26.

To investigate the economic status of racial minorities, Katzman utilizes an economic model developed to explain the economic condition of immigrants. The author concludes that the lower occupational status, income, and employment rate of blacks may be either the result of preferences by the minorities or discrimination.

Kessler, Matthew A. "Economic Status of Non-White Workers, 1955-62." MONTHLY LABOR REVIEW 86 (July 1963): 1-9. Tables.

Kessler compares relative changes in the white and nonwhite occupational distribution over the period 1955-62. Blacks increased their representation among factory operatives but made few incursions upon the ranks of technical and professional workers.

Kifer, Allen. "Changing Patterns of Negro Employment." INDUSTRIAL RE-
LATIONS 3 (May 1964): 23-36.

 Kifer traces the occupational status of blacks from the 1890s through
 the 1950s. Blacks have been confined to low paying jobs and have
 only experienced improvement during periods of extensive labor
 shortages. Economic advancement has been transitory, fluctuating
 with the business cycle.

Killingsworth, Charles C. "Negroes in a Changing Labor Market." In JOBS
AND COLOR, pp. 49-75. Edited by Arthur M. Ross. New York: Harcourt,
Brace, and World, 1967.

 Killingsworth attributes the employment condition of blacks to
 structural problems as opposed to insufficiency of aggregate demand. Training and relocation programs are more effective than
 expansionary monetary and fiscal policies to increase black employment and improve the occupational distribution of blacks.

Kovarsky, Irving, and Albreckt, William. BLACK EMPLOYMENT: THE IMPACT
OF RELIGION, ECONOMIC THEORY, POLITICS, AND LAW. Ames: Iowa
State University Press, 1970. 152 p.

 The study's thesis is that the black's current economic condition is
 the result of religious, economic, political, and legal theories
 which obstructed the transition from slavery before and after the
 Civil War. Societal institutions must make concerted efforts to
 obliterate discrimination before economic equality will be attained
 for blacks.

Larner, Jeremy, and Howe, Irving, eds. POVERTY: VIEWS FROM THE LEFT.
New York: William Morrow and Co., 1968. 319 p.

Levenson, Bernard, and McDill, Mary S. "Vocational Graduates in Auto
Mechanics: A Follow-Up Study of Negro and White Youth." PHYLON 27
(Fourth Quarter, 1966): 347-57.

 Levenson and McDill conducted a longitudinal study of black and
 white graduates of two vocational high schools. Students were
 comparable in terms of educational achievement; the schools were
 of comparable academic quality. Still, a significant earnings differential exists between the blacks and whites. This earnings differential is attributed to discrimination.

Lyle, Jerolyn R. DIFFERENCES IN THE OCCUPATIONAL STANDING OF
BLACK WORKERS AMONG INDUSTRIES AND CITIES. Washington, D.C.:
U.S. Equal Employment Opportunity Commission, Office of Research and Re-
ports, 1970. 29 p.

 Lyle reports that the occupational distribution of black workers is
 more a function of the socioeconomic characteristics of the cities
 in which they reside than personal factors, such as level of edu-

cational attainment. The degree of housing integration is a better
predictor of occupational distribution than differences in the unemployment rate among cities. Black women tend to have a better
occupational distribution in cities with low rates of population increase through migration.

Madden, J. Patrick. "Poverty by Color and Residence—Projections to 1975
and 1980." AMERICAN JOURNAL OF AGRICULTURAL ECONOMICS 50
(December 1968): 1399–412.

Madden projects a relative decline in rural poverty and an increase
in urban poverty between 1975 and 1980. Blacks and other nonwhites will experience a reduction in absolute poverty, but relative
poverty will only improve slightly if the trends of the 1960s continue into the 1970s and 1980s. A problem with this projection
is that it assumes migration from rural to urban areas will continue
at the pace experienced in the past. This assumption is questionable in view of empirical evidence in the early 1970s.

Maddox, James G. THE ADVANCING SOUTH: MANPOWER PROSPECTS
AND PROBLEMS. New York: Twentieth Century Fund, 1967. 276 p. Tables.

Maddox contends that the transformation of jobs in southern industry from low to higher skill requirements and the failure of the
region's educational system to adequately prepare blacks for the
higher skilled jobs are the most important factors retarding the
improvement of the black's economic condition in the "New South."

Marshall, F. Ray. LABOR IN THE SOUTH. Cambridge, Mass.: Harvard
University Press, 1967. 406 p. Tables.

Marshall describes the employment condition and obstacles to improvement in the status of black labor in the South.

_____. THE NEGRO WORKER. New York: Random House, 1967. 180 p.
Tables.

Marshall describes the status of black workers, with particular
emphasis upon those in labor unions, the factors determining that
condition, and prospects and policies for improvement. Black
employment prospects are viewed as highly contingent upon the
maintenance of full employment nationally as well as strong antidiscrimination efforts by the government.

Marshall, F. Ray, and Adams, Arvil Van. "Negro Employment in Memphis."
INDUSTRIAL RELATIONS 9 (May 1970): 308–23. Tables.

Institutional discrimination in Memphis hampers black employment
opportunities. Blacks do not have equal access to training, job
market information, and transportation. Employers have discriminated and taken little affirmative action.

Marshall, Harvey, Jr. "Black-White Economic Participation in Large U.S. Cities." AMERICAN JOURNAL OF ECONOMICS AND SOCIOLOGY 31 (October 1972): 361-72. Tables.

Marshall identifies factors which may account for the unemployment rates and labor force participation rates of blacks. Educational and occupational differences between blacks and whites and the degree of residential segregation do not explain the unemployment and participation differentials between the two groups. Although discrimination appears to be the major determinant, there is no way to test this hypothesis.

Martin, Walter T. "Occupational Differential by Color: Age-Sex-Specific Variations for Occupational Categories." POPULATION INDEX 33 (July/September 1967): 336. Tables.

Martin catalogues the occupational distribution of the American labor force by race, age, and sex. Relative to participation in the total labor force, blacks comprise a smaller proportion of higher-paying, higher-status occupations than whites.

Meier, August, and Rudwick, Elliott M. FROM PLANTATION TO GHETTO. New York: Hill and Wang, 1966. 280 p.

Meier and Rudwick trace the movement of blacks between two sharply contrasting environments, the plantation and the ghetto, and provide an understanding of the origins and nature of economic and social institutions which confront blacks.

Miller, Herman P. "Poverty and the Negro." In POVERTY IN AMERICA; BOOK OF READINGS, pp. 160-76. Edited by Louis A. Ferman, et al. Ann Arbor: University of Michigan Press, 1968. Tables.

Miller provides an excellent statistical profile of the black poor in terms of geographic distribution, family structure, and occupational distribution.

Muller, Andre L. "Economic Growth and Minorities." AMERICAN JOURNAL OF ECONOMICS AND SOCIOLOGY 26 (July 1967): 225-30. Tables.

Muller observes that in recent years the economic position of blacks has improved faster than that of whites. This improvement, however, has progressed at a slower rate than incomes.

National Commission on Urban Problems. "The Urban Setting: Population, Poverty, Race." In BUILDING THE AMERICAN CITY: REPORT OF THE NATIONAL COMMISSION ON URBAN PROBLEMS TO THE CONGRESS AND TO THE PRESIDENT OF THE UNITED STATES, pp. 40-55. 1969. Tables. Sold by Government Printing Office.

The Commission makes projections for total population, percentage of minorities, degree of urbanization, and income distribution for 1985. Little improvements for the minority poor is foreseen. Although institutional changes would alter this prognosis, they are disregarded because they are unpredictable.

Newhouse, Joseph P. "A Simple Hypothesis of Income Distribution." JOURNAL OF HUMAN RESOURCES 6 (Winter 1971): 51-74.

Newhouse finds that the industrial composition of a geographical area appears to be the prime determinant of its income distribution and far outweighs factors such as age, educational distribution, and discrimination.

Newman, Dorothy K. THE NEGROES IN THE UNITED STATES: THEIR ECO-NOMIC AND SOCIAL SITUATION. Washington, D.C.: U.S. Department of Labor, 1966. 241 p. Tables and charts. Sold by Government Printing Office.

Newman describes the social and economic situation of blacks, and enumerates their participation in government programs to aid vet-erans and the general populace. Most of the data provided in this volume, however, is out of date. The sources of information are of particular value to the researcher.

Niemi, Albert W. "Changes in Racially Structured Employment Patterns in the Northeast and South, 1940-60." AMERICAN JOURNAL OF ECONOMICS AND SOCIOLOGY 31 (April 1972): 171-79. Tables.

Niemi compares differences in the occupational structure among whites and blacks in the North and South. In both the Northeast and the South, he found that the 1940 employment patterns were drawn on very sharp racial lines, and stratification of employment was much more rigid for female blacks than for males. Over the period from 1940 to 1960, a moderate shift occurred in the North-east but did not occur in the South.

O'Boyle, Edward J. "Job Tenure: How it Relates to Race and Age." MONTH-LY LABOR REVIEW 92 (September 1969): 16-23.

O'Boyle observes that job tenure is positively correlated with age and does not differ significantly among races. The high labor turnover rates encountered by black youth is more a function of age than of race.

Offner, Paul. "Labor Force Participation in the Ghetto." JOURNAL OF HUMAN RESOURCES 7 (Fall 1972): 460-81. Tables.

Offner reports that a major factor contributing to ghetto employ-ment problems is the poor location of ghettos relative to job loca-tions. Labor supply is depressed in the ghetto for the prime age group, but not for teenagers and older people. After controlling for demographic, social, and economic characteristics, Offner finds that prime age people in the ghetto have depressed participation rates partly as a result of the shortage of jobs there.

O'Neill, Dave M. "The Effect of Discrimination on Earnings: Evidence from Military Test Score Results." JOURNAL OF HUMAN RESOURCES 5 (Fall 1970): 475-86. Tables.

The military test score performance of black and white youth was used to estimate the importance of discrimination on earnings. About half the black-white income differential was attributed to discrimination. Unlike most others, this study is of particular interest because it differentiates between quantity and quality of education when attempting to determine the effects of discrimination.

Orshansky, Mollie. "Who's Who among the Poor: A Demographic View of Poverty." SOCIAL SECURITY BULLETIN 28 (July 1965): 3-33. Tables.

Orshansky provides a statistical description of the composition of the poor as defined by the minimum income levels of the United States Social Security Administration. She also provides data on race, age, sex, and employment status.

Peck, Sidney M. "The Economic Situation of Negro Labor." In THE NEGRO AND THE AMERICAN LABOR MOVEMENT, pp. 210-28. Edited by Julius Jacobson. New York: Doubleday and Co., 1968.

Peck observes that the vast majority of black workers are employed in blue-collar and service industry jobs. These jobs are becoming increasingly marginal, while the proportion of blacks comprising them is also increasing. Moreover, twice as many blacks as whites are unemployed, no matter what the occupation, educational level, sex, or age.

Piore, Michael J. "Negro Workers in the Mississippi Delta." MONTHLY LABOR REVIEW 91 (April 1968): 23-25.

Piore describes the condition of black workers in the declining regional economy of the Mississippi Delta. Industry in that area has encountered difficulties securing workers willing to submit to the discipline of the factory despite the high unemployment and subemployment in the agricultural sector of the region.

Rasmussen, D. W. "Discrimination and the Income of Non-White Males." AMERICAN JOURNAL OF ECONOMICS AND SOCIOLOGY 30 (October 1971): 377-82. Tables.

Rasmussen estimates that the removal of all discrimination in the non-South and South would increase nonwhite income by 17 and 45 percent respectively. While government policy could beneficially focus on the quality of nonwhite education, white prejudice is the largest barrier to equality for nonwhite income.

_____. "A Note on the Relative Income of Nonwhite Men." QUARTERLY JOURNAL OF ECONOMICS 84 (February 1970): 168-72. Tables.

Rasmussen contends that the recent decline in the nonwhite-white income ratio reflects cyclical impacts rather than a secular trend. The decline may reflect a reduction in the migration of nonwhites from the South to the North rather than a decline in the propensity of whites to discriminate.

Reder, Melvin. "Human Capital and Economic Discrimination." In HUMAN RESOURCES AND ECONOMIC WELFARE: ESSAYS IN HONOR OF ELI GINZ-BERG, pp. 72-86. Edited by Svar Berg. New York: Columbia University Press, 1972.

Reder observes that the cost to the employer of acquiring informa-tion on the location and abilities of minority group workers is gen-erally not considered in employment and income studies. Subse-quently the low proportion of minority employees is often inter-preted as discrimination.

Roberts, Merkley. "Some Factors Affecting Employment and Earnings of Dis-advantaged Youths." INDUSTRIAL AND LABOR RELATIONS REVIEW 25 (April 1972): 376-82.

The earnings and employment of black males after application to a preapprenticeship outreach program are dependent variables in a regression analysis. Fourteen independent variables are utilized. One of the variables, prior work experience, was found to have a negative effect on earnings. All other variables were below the 10 percent level of significance.

Ross, Arthur M. "The Negro in the American Economy." In EMPLOYMENT, RACE, AND POVERTY, pp. 1-23. Edited by Arthur M. Ross and Herbert Hill. New York: Harcourt, Brace, and World, 1967.

After examining time series data on the black's economic status, Ross reaches the conclusion that the major reason for low black incomes is not higher unemployment but the concentration fo black workers in low paying jobs. The greatest occupational progress for blacks has occured in periods of high labor demand and low unemployment.

Rothwell, Donnie. "Counting People, Reaching People." COMMUNITIES IN ACTION 3 (February/March 1968): 3-7.

Rothwell contends that the failure of the United States Bureau of the Census to count appreciable numbers of blacks results in serious deficiencies in research and policy.

Ruchlin, Hirsch S. "Education as a Labor Market Variable." INDUSTRIAL RELATIONS 10 (October 1971): 287-300. Tables.

Ruchlin observes that because clerical, sales, and service occupa-tions require greater contact between the employee and the con-sumer, discrimination there has a greater impact than in industries with less interpersonal contact. The passage of the 1964 Civil Rights

Law does not appear to have led to increased educational requirements but in fact has led to a lowering of educational requirements,
thereby decreasing employment discrimination.

Satter, David A. "West Side Story: Home Is Where the Welfare Check Comes."
THE NEW REPUBLIC 155 (July 1966): 15-19.

Satter describes the slums of West Side Chicago as inhabited by
welfare recipients whose lack of respect for the law is nurtured
by the injustices of the welfare system.

Saunders, Robert J., and Coccari, Ronald L. "Racial Earnings Differentials:
Some Economics Factors." AMERICAN JOURNAL OF ECONOMICS AND SO-
CIOLOGY 23 (July 1973): 225-33.

Saunders and Coccari find that education differentials and local
labor market conditions are significant determinants of the black-
white income differential. By expanding educational opportunities
for blacks and increasing demand for labor, the income differential
will narrow. Intraindustry earnings differentials are greater in areas
where blacks are a relatively large proportion of the population.
This suggests that blacks should relocate.

Schiller, Bradley R. "Class Discrimination Vs. Racial Discrimination." THE
REVIEW OF ECONOMICS AND STATISTICS 53 (August 1971): 263-69. Tables.

Schiller examines the relative socioeconomic achievements of black
and white children who were reared in families receiving public
assistance. The educational and early occupational handicaps imposed upon lower class youth by their impoverished economic origins are the same kind and perhaps quantitatively as important as
handicaps attributable to racial discrimination. Class discrimination is as important as racial discrimination in limiting the attain-
ments of poor youth.

_____. THE ECONOMICS OF POVERTY AND DISCRIMINATION. Englewood
Cliffs, N.J.: Prentice-Hall, 1972. 199 p.

Schiller disputes assumptions of welfare reform proposals that the
poor prefer welfare to work, that jobs will provide economic security, and that job opportunities for the poor do exist. A negative
income tax plan is favored over the Family Assistance Plan because it
would be more universal and implies less government control over
the behavior of the poor. Monetary and fiscal policies, training
programs, and public service employment are interdependent, and
their uses must be coordinated in order to reduce poverty. Equal
opportunity policies can reduce poverty by providing blacks with
access to educational credentials and improve access to higher
paying jobs.

Schmidt, Fred H. "Los Angeles: Show, Little Substance." INDUSTRIAL RE-
LATIONS 9 (May 1970): 340-55. Tables.

Since the Watts riot of 1965, a number of government sponsored training programs were initiated to reduce the unemployment and improve the occupational distribution of blacks. Their success has been minimal as the feeling of urgency about removing the causes of civil disorders has lessened, and the pace of economic growth has slowed.

Schuchter, Arnold. WHITE POWER/BLACK FREEDOM: PLANNING THE FUTURE OF URBAN AMERICA. Boston: Beacon Press, 1968. 650 p.

Shaffer, Helen B. "Negroes in the Economy." EDITORIAL RESEARCH REPORTS 1 (March 8, 1967): 183-200. Tables.

Shaffer assesses the economic condition of blacks. The economic benefits accruing to both blacks and whites from equal employment opportunity include higher national income, greater tax revenues, and lower welfare costs.

Shapiro, Theresa. A STUDY OF BLACK MALE PROFESSIONALS IN INDUSTRY. Washington, D.C.: U.S. Department of Labor. 22 p.

Shapiro reports that between 1966 and 1970 the proportion of blacks in professional, technical, and managerial positions doubled. This rate corresponds to a doubling of black college graduates between 1962 and 1972.

Sheppard, Harold L., and Striner, Herbert E. CIVIL RIGHTS, EMPLOYMENT, AND THE SOCIAL STATUS OF AMERICAN NEGROES. Kalamazoo, Mich.: W. E. Upjohn Institute for Employment Research, 1966. 85 p.

Siegel, P. M. "On the Cost of Being a Negro." SOCIOLOGICAL INQUIRY 35 (Winter 1965): 41-52. Tables.

By using the United States Department of Census data on income for various educational and occupational groups, estimates are made of the dollar value of discrimination against blacks. Overall, Siegel estimates the cost of being black to be approximately $1,000 per year, which makes the return on educational investment appreciably less for blacks than for whites.

Silberman, Charles E. "Let's Talk about the Real World." AMERICAN CHILD 46 (November 1964): 4-8.

The unemployment rate for black teenagers is usually in the 50 percent range. Silberman attributes this high unemployment incidence to changing job requirements, inadequate education, and lack of motivation.

Simon, Julian L. "The Effect of Fixed-Wage Raises on Discriminated-Against Minorities." INDUSTRIAL AND LABOR RELATIONS REVIEW 21 (October 1967): 96-97.

Simon assumes that employers prefer to hire white over black workers, if they are compelled by either a union or a law to pay the same wage to both. The supply of white labor services being offered at low wages is less than that for blacks. He demonstrates graphically that an increase in the wage will reduce the number of blacks hired and increase the number of whites employed.

Smith, Ralph E. "A Job Search--Turnover Analysis of the Black-White Unemployment Ratio." In PROCEEDINGS OF THE TWENTY-THIRD ANNUAL WINTER MEETING, pp. 76-86. Edited by Gerald G. Somers. Madison, Wis.: Industrial Relations Research Association, 1971.

The reason why the unemployment rate for black males is double that for whites is because the black separation rate is double that for whites. Low wages, lower seniority, and easier access by blacks to jobs with less stability account for the higher black separation rate.

Smith, Stanley M. "The Older Rural Negro." In OLDER RURAL AMERICANS, pp. 262-80. Edited by Grant E. Youmans. Lexington: University of Kentucky Press, 1967.

Smith describes the social and economic condition of elderly rural blacks and their urban counterparts. While incomes are lower in the country, social conditions are more stable than in the cities.

Sorkin, Alan L. "Education, Occupation, and Income of Nonwhite Women." JOURNAL OF NEGRO EDUCATION 41 (Fall 1972): 43-51.

Sorkin reports that the income gap between white and nonwhite women declined between 1950 and 1970 largely because nonwhite women with a college degree earn more than their white counterparts. Black female teachers earn more than white female teachers-- the largest single occupation of female college graduates.

Stern, Sol. "Trouble in All America City." NEW YORK TIMES MAGAZINE, July 10, 1966, pp. 21-29.

Stern describes the socioeconomic condition of blacks in Oakland, California.

Stiglitz, Joseph E. "Approaches to the Economics of Discrimination." AMERICAN ECONOMIC REVIEW 63 (May 1973): 287-95. Tables.

Stiglitz examines a number of theories on discrimination including Gary Becker's discrimination-preference trade model theory, the efficiency wage model, and labor market disequilibrium models. It is not clear that any of these models provides satisfactory explanations of black-white income differentials. The economic consequences of alternative policies are probably less important in the assessment of their desirability than political, social, and philosophical considerations.

Struyk, Raymond J. "Explaining Variations in the Hourly Wage Rates of Urban Minority Group Females." JOURNAL OF HUMAN RESOURCES 8 (Summer 1973): 349-64. Tables.

Struyk hypothesizes that the number of hours worked by urban minority females determines their hourly wage rate, given employers' preferences for full time workers. Because of the low amount of human capital they possess, nonwhite females qualify for only low paying jobs. The low hourly wage rate they receive increases the relative value of house work, which should cause a substitution of house work for labor force participation. However, this is not the case. The need for a minimum level of income is the deciding factor in determining labor force participation.

Taylor, David P. "Discrimination and Occupational Wage Differences in the Market for Unskilled Labor." INDUSTRIAL AND LABOR RELATIONS REVIEW 21 (April 1968): 375-90. Tables.

In a survey of eighty businesses in the Chicago area, Taylor finds that employment discrimination against blacks occurs even in un-skilled occupations. The two occupations examined are material handler and janitor. Less wage and employment discrimination occurs in janitorial work, a dead-end occupation, than in material handling, an occupation which affords some opportunity for upward mobility.

Thurow, Lester C. "The Causes of Poverty." QUARTERLY JOURNAL OF ECONOMICS 81 (February 1967): 39-57.

Thurow estimates the relative importance of various characteristics of the poor. Full employment and the maintenance of a high rate of economic growth are viewed as necessary preconditions for the success of government sponsored manpower training programs.

_____. POVERTY AND DISCRIMINATION. Washington, D.C.: Brookings Institution, 1969. 214 p. Tables.

Thurow examines the incidence of poverty both cross sectionally and over a period of time, the role of human capital in determining income distributions, economic effects of various forms of discrimina-tion against nonwhites, and policy implications. Nonwhites are more likely than whites to be poor. The marginal value of education, especially at higher levels of schooling, is less for nonwhites than for whites, while estimates show that the marginal value of experi-ence is also less for at least fifteen years after entry into the labor force.

United States Bureau of the Census. THE SOCIAL AND ECONOMIC STATUS OF THE BLACK POPULATION IN THE UNITED STATES. Current Population Reports, Special Studies, Series P-23, no. 48. Washington, D.C.: U.S. Government Printing Office, 1973. 146 p. Tables.

The report provides data on population growth, composition, and

distribution, income, labor force participation, occupational distribution, unemployment, family composition and nature, housing and
health conditions, voting behavior, and elected officials with a
special section on low-income areas in selected cities.

United States Civil Service Commission. STUDY OF MINORITY GROUP EM-
PLOYMENT IN THE FEDERAL GOVERNMENT. Washington, D.C.: 1965.
193 p. Tables. Sold by Government Printing Office.

Minority workers are concentrated in low-paying, low-status jobs
within the federal government. Upward occupational mobility for
minorities is limited.

United States Commission on Civil Rights. REPORTS ON APPRENTICESHIP.
Washington, D.C.: 1964. 158 p. Sold by Government Printing Office.

The report details the extent of minority participation in apprenticeship programs conducted in nine states. Blacks comprise a proportion of apprentices which is far below their representation in the
general population.

United States Departments of Commerce and Labor. SOCIAL AND ECONOMIC
CONDITIONS OF NEGROES IN THE UNITED STATES. Washington, D.C.:
Bureau of the Census and Bureau of Labor Statistics, 1967. 97 p. Tables.
Sold by Government Printing Office.

This report provides a statistical portrait of black America based
upon special government census studies, and includes data on incomes, employment, occupational structure, housing, and education.

United States Department of Labor. BLACK AMERICANS--A DECADE OF OC-
CUPATIONAL CHANGE. Washington, D.C.: U.S. Government Printing
Office. 22 p. Charts.

Between the 1960s and 1970s, the proportion of blacks in white-
collar, craftsmen, and operative occupations increased by about
10 percent. Because the gap in educational attainment between
blacks and whites is narrowing among the young, the prospects for
improvement in the future are encouraging.

_____. THE FACTS OF POVERTY IN NEW YORK CITY. New York: Bureau
of Labor Statistics, March 1965. 21 p. Tables.

The report provides a statistical description of the poor by race,
sex, and age in New York City.

United States Department of Labor and United States Department of Commerce.
SOCIAL AND ECONOMIC STATUS OF NEGROES IN THE UNITED STATES.
Washington, D.C.: U.S. Department of Labor and Commerce, 1969. 96 p.
Tables. Sold by Government Printing Office.

Improvements in the socioeconomic condition of blacks were recorded during the 1960s, but wide differences between blacks and whites remain.

United States Equal Employment Opportunity Commission. WHITE COLLAR EMPLOYMENT IN 100 MAJOR NEW YORK CITY CORPORATIONS. Washington, D.C.: 1968. 29 p. Tables.

Black and Puerto Rican employment in white-collar jobs in New York City is increasing but tends to be confined to lower echelon positions.

_____ . WHITE COLLAR EMPLOYMENT IN THE NEW YORK CITY FINANCIAL COMMUNITY. Washington, D.C.: 1968. 33 p. Tables.

The employment of blacks and Puerto Ricans in banking, insurance companies, and brokerage houses located in New York City is increasing but generally confined to nonmanagement positions.

_____ . WHITE COLLAR EMPLOYMENT IN THE NEW YORK CITY COMMUNICATIONS INDUSTRY. Washington, D.C.: 1968. 27 p. Tables.

Black and Puerto Rican employment in advertising, publishing, and broadcasting firms located in New York City is increasing but tends to be concentrated in lower echelon positions.

Via, Emory F. "Discrimination, Integration, and Job Equality." MONTHLY LABOR REVIEW 91 (March 1968): 82-89. Tables.

Via observes that racial integration of employment is occurring in the South, but at a slow pace. This discussion includes the roles of government, employers, and unions in accelerating that pace.

Wachtel, Dawn. THE NEGRO AND DISCRIMINATION IN EMPLOYMENT. Ann Arbor, Mich.: Institute of Labor and Industrial Relations, 1965. 112 p. Tables.

Wachtel describes the economic condition of black workers and how that condition is perpetuated by discriminatory employer and union practices.

Walter, Ingo, and Kramer, John E. "Political Autonomy and Economic Dependence in an All-Negro Municipality." AMERICAN JOURNAL OF ECONOMICS AND SOCIOLOGY 28 (July 1969): 225-48. Tables.

The economic growth of a small, all-black town appears to hinge upon the acquisition of academic and technical skills by a work force that must function almost entirely in the outside environment. The key factor is an improved educational system, tightly run and competently staffed. As earning power improves, so too will housing and the educational system.

Weaver, Jerry L. "Educational Attainment and Economic Success: Some Notes on a Ghetto Study." JOURNAL OF NEGRO EDUCATION 40 (Spring 1971): 153-58.

Weaver finds no significant correlation between educational attainment and unemployment among blacks in Long Beach, California. In addition, school curriculum major and educational attainment bear no significant correlation with incomes received.

Weiss, Leonard, and Williamson, Jeffrey G. "Black Education, Earnings, and Interregional Migration: Some New Evidence." AMERICAN ECONOMIC REVIEW 62 (June 1972): 372-83. Tables.

Weiss and Williamson report that the inferiority of southern black schools has little impact upon the economic condition of northern migrants. The effect of the large urban ghetto environment is more harmful to black economic progress than southern origin. Increased investment in education will generate economic progress for blacks.

Welch, Finis. "Black-White Differences in Return to Schooling." AMERICAN ECONOMIC REVIEW 63 (December 1973): 393-407. Tables.

Between 1959 and 1966 the average earnings of blacks relative to whites rose rapidly. Much of this gain is associated with tightening labor markets, while the narrowing of the difference in years of schooling completed between whites and blacks is also a factor. In 1959, white high school graduates worked 15 to 20 percent more time than blacks. In 1966, this difference fell to 2 percent.

_____. "Labor-Market Discrimination: An Interpretation of Income Differences in the Rural South." JOURNAL OF POLITICAL ECONOMY 75 (June 1967): 225-40. Tables.

According to Welch, integration increases the productivity of workers as a consequence of the complementary relationship between workers of different educational backgrounds, but results in other inefficiencies since the productivity of a worker may decline when working alongside a worker of a different race. As blacks increase the number of years spent in school, the impact of inferior quality schooling and market discrimination increases.

Wetzel, James R., and Holland, Susan S. "Poverty Areas of Our Major Cities." MONTHLY LABOR REVIEW 89 (October 1966): 1105-10.

Wetzel and Holland observe that the unemployment rate for whites and blacks in poverty areas of major cities is more than double the national rate. Among black teenagers the unemployment rate is about 50 percent.

Williams, Walter. "Cleveland's Crisis Ghetto." TRANS-ACTION 4 (September 1967): 33-37.

Williams describes the condition of blacks in Cleveland, Ohio.

Winegarden, C. R. "Barriers to Black Employment in White Collar Jobs: A Quantitative Approach." REVIEW OF BLACK POLITICAL ECONOMY 2 (Spring 1972): 13-24.

> Winegarden reports that blacks appear to gain greater accessibility to white-collar jobs in regions of the country where they constitute a high proportion of the total population. The major determinant appears to be the difference in years of educational attainment between blacks and whites. But even if education was equalized, underrepresentation of blacks would still exist. Discrimination appears to be a dominant factor.

Wright, Nathan. "The Economics of Race." AMERICAN JOURNAL OF ECONOMICS AND SOCIOLOGY 26 (January 1967): 1-12. Tables.

> Wright views the so-called progress of blacks since World War II in its economic context: the improvement is not apparent.

Chapter 2

THE PSYCHOLOGY OF RACE

Chapter 2

THE PSYCHOLOGY OF RACE

Acuff, Joe M. "Meeting the Challenge of Training the Hard Core Unemployed." TRAINING AND DEVELOPMENT JOURNAL 23 (July 1969): 42-43.

Acuff prescribes dedication and an overall approach in order to succeed in employment of the disadvantaged. The problems of the disadvantaged are many faceted and include inadequate education, poor self-concept, and lack of employment discipline.

Aiken, Michael, and Ferman, Louis A. "The Social and Political Reactions of Older Negroes to Unemployment." PHYLON 27 (1966): 333-46.

The perception of personal failure due to unemployment among blacks leads to alienation from the political system. In order to combat unemployment, emphasis must be placed upon job training.

Allport, Gordon W. THE NATURE OF PREJUDICE. New York: Doubleday and Co., 1958. 496 p.

Allport disagrees with the view that government cannot legislate against prejudice even though enforceability of antidiscrimination laws is difficult. The very existence of such laws does affect societal attitudes and actions and eventually may reduce prejudice.

Baird, Virginia W. "Employing the Disadvantaged Fraught with Challenges." TRAINING AND DEVELOPMENT JOURNAL 23 (July 1969): 44-46.

Baird enumerates problems of health, education, attitude, and aptitude confronted by those employing the disadvantaged. He concludes that the challenge is worth undertaking, on the basis of social responsibility as well as the profitability for the firm.

Baughman, E. Earl. BLACK AMERICANS: A PSYCHOLOGICAL ANALYSIS. New York: Academic Press, 1971. 113 p.

Bloom, Richard, et al. "Race and Social Class as Separate Factors Related to Social Environment." AMERICAN JOURNAL OF SOCIOLOGY 70 (January 1965): 471-76. Tables.

The authors test eleven dependent variables on groups of white and black children and conclude that class is more important than race in determining social environment. Black attitudes toward the means for economic achievement appear to be more a function of socio-economic class than race.

Brink, William, and Harris, Louis. BLACK AND WHITE: A STUDY OF U.S. RACIAL ATTITUDES TODAY. New York: Simon and Schuster, 1967. 285 p.

Brink and Harris trace the changes in racial attitudes in whites and blacks since the 1940s as determined by public opinion surveys.

Clark, Kenneth. "Sex, Status, and Underemployment of the Negro Male." In EMPLOYMENT, RACE, AND POVERTY, pp. 138-48. Edited by Arthur M. Ross and Herbert Hill. New York: Harcourt, Brace, and World, 1967.

Black family structure suffers a debilitating blow because of employment discrimination against the black male and the better employment opportunities for the black female.

Clinard, Marshall B. "The Role of Motivation and Self-Image in Social Change in Slum Areas." In PSYCHOLOGICAL FACTORS IN POVERTY, pp. 326-47. Edited by Vernon L. Allen. Chicago: Markham Publishing Co., 1970.

Clinard states that the reason programs to improve the socioeconomic condition of slum dwellers are unsuccessful is that the poor lack the motivation to take advantage of presented opportunities. Self-image and achievement motivation are necessary prerequisites.

Colfax, J. David, and Sternberg, Susan Frankel. "The Perpetuation of Racial Stereotypes: Blacks in Mass Circulation Magazine Advertisements." PUBLIC OPINION QUARTERLY 36 (Spring 1972): 8-18.

Deutsch, Martin, and Brown, Bert. "Social Influence in Negro-White Intelligence Differences." SOCIAL ISSUES 20 (April 1964): 27.

Deutsch and Brown attribute the relatively low score of nonwhites on standardized tests to environmental factors which affect self-concept and motivation.

Dreger, Ralph M., and Miller, Kent S. "Recent Research in Psychological Comparisons of Negroes and Whites in the United States." Atlanta, Ga.: Southern Psychological Association, 1966. Mimeographed.

Dreger and Miller survey fifty research studies on racial differences. They challenge the methods employed in much of the research and enumerate factors accounting for racial differences.

Erickson, Edsel L., et al. "Differences between Economically Disadvantaged Students Who Volunteer and Do Not Volunteer for Economic Opportunity Programs." JOURNAL OF HUMAN RESOURCES 4 (Winter 1969): 76-83. Tables.

Students who volunteer for economic opportunity programs have lower
school achievement levels, lower academic support from parents and
friends, lower self-conceptions of academic ability, lower educational aspirations, and lower occupational plan levels than those
who do not. Only in the area of teacher support for academic
achievement did volunteers exceed the nonvolunteers. No difference in academic ability existed between volunteers and nonvolunteers.

Farley, Reynolds. "Family Types and Family Headship: A Comparison of Trends
among Blacks and Whites." JOURNAL OF HUMAN RESOURCES 6 (Summer
1971): 275-96. Tables.

Farley examines the hypotheses that the decrease in the proportion
of husband-wife black families in recent decades has led to a
breakdown of the black family, and that the economic status of
black men accounts for the instability of black families. A growing proportion of adult blacks are heading families, and socioeconomic status is positively related to the likelihood that a man will
head a husband-wife family.

Gans, Herbert J. "Negro Problems and White Fantasies." THE URBAN RE-
VIEW 1 (December 1966): 2-3.

Gans asserts that whites are too easily impressed by the rhetoric of
black militants and have encouraged programs designed to meet
their demands, while ignoring the needs and aspirations of the
majority of blacks. The needs of both poor whites and blacks
should not be ignored.

Ganz, Samuel. "The Social Roots of Unemployment." In THE MANPOWER
REVOLUTION, pp. 155-75. Edited by Garth L. Mangum. New York: Doubleday and Co., 1965.

Motivation toward employment on the part of many unemployed and
their children is hampered because long-term unemployment and
relegation to dead-end jobs discourages workers from exploring career opportunities.

Gowan, John C., and Demos, George D., eds. THE DISADVANTAGED AND
POTENTIAL DROPOUT. Springfield, III.: Charles C. Thomas, Publisher, 1966.
624 p.

The volume contains essays on the problems faced by educators in
assisting culturally disadvantaged students.

Greenberg, Edward S. "Black Children and the Political System." PUBLIC
OPINION QUARTERLY 34 (Fall 1970): 333-45.

Greenberg compares the attitudes of black and white children toward
the American political system and finds that dissatisfaction among
lower socioeconomic class blacks is greater than that for whites of

the same class, and greater for both blacks and whites in higher classes. He also concludes that disaffection increases with age.

Grigsby, Eugene III. "Stratification in American Society: A Case for Reappraisal." JOURNAL OF BLACK STUDIES 2 (December 1971): 157-69.

The values of American society, according to Grigsby, have rationalized and protected a class structure which has relegated blacks to the lowest position.

Gruber, Murray. "The Nonculture of Poverty among Black Youths." SOCIAL WORK 17 (May 1972): 50-58.

According to Gruber's survey, black youth from poor families have higher income aspirations than might be expected in view of the cycle of poverty.

Hare, Nathan. "The Sociological Study of Racial Conflict." PHYLON 33 (Spring 1972): 27-31.

Hare believes that sociologists are incapable of studying racial conflicts due to bias and value judgments reflective of white middle-class society.

Harrell, David Edwin, Jr. WHITE SECTS AND BLACK MEN IN THE RECENT SOUTH. Nashville, Tenn.: Vanderbilt University Press, 1971. 161 p.

Low socioeconomic class whites in the South and religious sects in which they predominate appear to harbor less prejudice toward blacks than higher-class whites.

Hess, Robert D. "The Transmission of Cognitive Strategies in Poor Families: The Socialization of Apathy and Underachievement." In PSYCHOLOGICAL FACTORS IN POVERTY, pp. 72-92. Edited by Vernon L. Allen. Chicago: Markham Publishing Co., 1970.

Children from poor families learn patterns of behavior at home which are not conducive to adaptation in school. In Hess's view, these patterns of behavior are the result of the social structure of the community in which the poor reside.

Hill, Richard J., and Larson, Calvin J. "Differential Ghetto Organization." PHYLON 32 (Fall 1971): 302-11.

Upon comparing social characteristics of blacks residing in different poverty areas of a city, it is inappropriate to characterize black slum dwellers as a homogeneous class.

Himes, Joseph S. "Some Work Related Cultural Deprivations of Lower-Class Negro Youths." In NEGROES AND JOBS, pp. 187-93. Edited by Louis A. Ferman. Ann Arbor: University of Michigan Press, 1968.

Because of lack of contact with workers in high-paying, high-status jobs, whatever knowledge and skill many black youths possess, they do not exhibit the fringe cultural characteristics in speech pattern and demeanor which white employers associate with on-the-job success. Because of these differences in speech pattern and demeanor, employers tend to view many black youths as unqualified for jobs despite their knowledge and skill.

Hodge, Robert W., and Treiman, Donald J. "Occupational Mobility and Attitudes toward Negroes." AMERICAN SOCIOLOGICAL REVIEW 31 (February 1966): 93-102.

Hodge and Treiman assess the role of social-class aspirations of whites in forming attitudes toward blacks.

Horton, John. "Time and Cool People." TRANS-ACTION 3 (April 1967): 5-12.

Horton examines the attitudes and aspirations of lower-socioeconomic class blacks and provides an understanding of the difficulties they confront in employment.

Jacob, Herbert. "Black and White Perceptions of Justice in the City." LAW AND SOCIETY REVIEW 6 (August 1971): 69-90.

Katz, Irwin, and Gurin, Patricia, eds. RACE AND THE SOCIAL SCIENCES. New York: Basic Books, 1969. 387 p.

Eight social scientists examine the state of research in their fields as it applies to the problem of racial inequality. Contents include James J. Coleman, "Race Relations and Social Change"; Herbert H. Hyman, "Social Psychology and Race Relations"; Irwin Katz and Patricia Gurin, "Race Relations and the Social Sciences"; Charles [G.] Killingsworth, "Jobs and Income for Negroes"; Donald Matthews, "Political Science Research on Race"; Karl E. Taeuber, "Negro Population and Housing: Demographic Aspects of a Social Accounting Scheme."

Keig, Norman G. "The Occupational Aspirations and Labor Force Experience of Negro Youth--A Case Study." AMERICAN JOURNAL OF ECONOMICS AND SOCIOLOGY 28 (April 1969): 113-30.

Keig finds a wide disparity between the occupational aspirations and labor force experience for black students at a southern school.

Kirchner, Wayne K., and Lucas, June A. "The Hard-Core in Training." TRAINING AND DEVELOPMENT JOURNAL 26 (May 1972): 34-37.

Dropouts from a preemployment training program generally scored higher on achievement tests than those completing the program. According to Kirchner and Lucas, the term "hard-core" is perhaps best applied to unmotivated individuals.

Klitgaard, Robert E. "Institutionalized Racism: An Analytic Approach." JOURNAL OF PEACE RESEARCH, no. 1 (1972), pp. 41-50.

> Racist responses by whites in employment and housing decisions may be rational responses on their part if blacks are not considered to be their equal. Klitgaard believes that the problem of two societies can be solved only when policy makers realize that racism can be a rational response.

Lenihan, Kenneth J. "Social Research on the Racial Crisis." THE PUBLIC OPINION QUARTERLY 29 (Fall 1965): 452-55.

> Surveys indicate that individual whites tend to view their racial attitudes as more liberal than those of the white community at large. This phenomenon has ramifications upon their behavior since they are afraid of offending their neighbors when racial issues arise.

Liebow, Elliot. TALLY'S CORNER. Boston: Little, Brown, and Co., 1966. 224 p.

> Liebow examines lower-socioeconomic black men in Washington, D.C. Most of the unemployed want to work. Those who don't are the most realistic about their employment prospects. Liebow identifies two of the problems as employer discrimination and inadequate education.

Macarov, David. "Culture of Poverty." In INCENTIVES TO WORK, pp. 109-22. San Francisco: Jossey-Bass, 1970.

> Macarov observes that there are basically two views of the poor's culture. One is that there are traits which are particular to the poor and require alteration before efforts to improve their economic status are undertaken. The other regards the poor as no different culturally than the affluent, and maintains that the poor will achieve a change in economic condition if presented with the opportunity for economic advancement.

Miller, Henry. "Social Work in the Black Ghetto: The New Colonialism." SOCIAL WORK 14 (July 1969): 65-76.

Milner, Richard B. "The Trickster, the Bad Nigga, and the New Urban Ethnography." URBAN LIFE AND CULTURE 1 (April 1972): 109-17.

> Milner criticizes traditional methods used in social science for the research of blacks: these methods are steeped in white middle-class value schemes.

Milutinovich, Jugoslav S. "Effects of Ghetto Life on Employees." URBAN AND SOCIAL CHANGE REVIEW 6 (Spring 1973): 69-72.

> Milutinovich views the prosperity of the community in which a worker resides as directly affecting his satisfaction with work, supervision, promotion, and overall job satisfaction.

Mizruchi, Ephraim Harold. "Aspirations and Poverty: A Neglected Aspect of Merton's Anomie." THE SOCIOLOGICAL QUARTERLY 8 (Autumn 1967): 439-46.

> The aspirations of the poor, according to Mizruchi, are such that even when provided with the opportunity, many are unwilling to attempt to achieve economic improvement.

Molotch, Harvey. "The Radicalization of Everyone?" In RACE, CHANGE, AND URBAN SOCIETY, pp. 517-60. Edited by Peter Orleans and William Russell Ellis, Jr. Beverly Hills, Calif.: Sage Publications, 1971.

> Molotch sees the attitudes of the white middle class toward issues like discrimination becoming increasingly liberal.

Morris, Frank L. "The Jensen Hypothesis: Was it the White Perspective or White Racism?" JOURNAL OF BLACK STUDIES 2 (March 1972): 371-86.

> Social scientists should not make inferences that depend on assumptions about black-white environmental comparability or on assumptions that interracial environmental differences can be measured with statistical confidence.

Murray, Paul. "Protest against the Legal Status of the Negro." THE ANNALS OF THE AMERICAN ACADEMY OF POLITICAL SCIENCES 357 (January 1965): 55-64.

> Mass protests against discrimination, according to Murray, are in a large part due to a change in the black self-concept.

Newman, Dorothy K. "The Negro's Journey to the City." REPORT CARD 14 (December 1965): Tables.

> Newman examines black attitudes toward economic achievement and concludes that they are directly related to opportunities. As opportunities improve so will attitudes.

Paige, Jeffrey M. "Changing Patterns of Anti-White Attitudes among Blacks." JOURNAL OF SOCIAL ISSUES 26 (Autumn 1970): 69-86.

> Traditionally, militant and higher-educated blacks expressed less hostility toward whites than lower-educated blacks. While integration was the general theme of black leadership in the past, separation and hostility toward white-dominated institutions is now more frequently its theme. Hostility among higher-educated, militant blacks appears to be increasing.

Pareek, Udaie. "Poverty and Motivation: Figure and Ground." In PSYCHOLOGICAL FACTORS IN POVERTY, pp. 300-317. Edited by Vernon L. Allen. Chicago: Markham Publishing Co., 1970.

> According to Pareek, the psychological nature of the poor is the effect of poverty, not the cause.

Perry, David C., and Feagin, Joe R. "Stereotyping in Black and White."
In PEOPLE AND POLITICS IN URBAN SOCIETY, pp. 433-63. Edited by Harlan
Hahn. Beverly Hills, Calif.: 1972.

   Perry and Feagin observe that social scientists compare the behavior
   of black ghetto residents with white middle-class values and treat
   deviations from those values as pathological.

Pettigrew, Thomas F. A PROFILE OF THE NEGRO AMERICAN. Princeton,
N.J.: D. Van Nostrand Co., 1964. 250 p.

   Pettigrew traces the condition of black Americans through history
   and observes that the obstacles posed by self-concept and motivation today are the direct result of historical subjugation. The
   circularity of economic status and motivation poses a dilemma that
   is difficult to break.

Porter, Judith D. R. BLACK CHILD, WHITE CHILD: THE DEVELOPMENT OF
RACIAL ATTITUDES. Cambridge, Mass.: Harvard University Press, 1971.
278 p.

   Porter examines the self-concept of black children and finds that
   socioeconomic class directly influences their self-concept. Desegregation in the schools does not appear to adversely affect the
   black child's self-concept as some critics of integration contend.

Rainwater, Lee. "The Lessons of Pruitt-Igoe." PUBLIC INTEREST 8 (Summer
1967): 116-26.

   Rainwater describes the decline of a federally sponsored high-rise
   apartment complex in St. Louis. He concludes that the poor cannot assume middle-class values while they are still poor. Massive
   income redistribution must be the initial step.

Rainwater, Lee, and Yancey, William L. THE MOYNIHAN REPORT AND THE
POLITICS OF CONTROVERSY. Cambridge, Mass.: M.I.T. Press, 1967. 493 p.

   This volume contains the text of the Moynihan Report which hy-
   pothesized that a major cause of black poverty is a dissolution of
   the black family. It also chronicles the debate prompted by this
   report.

Reubens, Edwin P. "Our Urban Ghettos in British Perspectives." URBAN
AFFAIRS QUARTERLY 6 (March 1971): 319-40.

   The most notable difference between racial minorities in the United
   States and Britain is the latter's lower unemployment rate. Yet
   social integration has not occurred in either country.

Rokeach, Milton, and Parker, Seymour. "Values as Social Indicators of Poverty
and Race Relations in America." ANNALS 388 (March 1970): 97-111.

   Rokeach and Parker dispute the contention that values leading to a self-perpetuating cycle of poverty are more frequently found among blacks than among whites.

Rose, Arnold M. and Rose, Carolyn B., eds. MINORITY PROBLEMS: A TEXTBOOK OF READINGS IN INTERGROUP RELATIONS. New York: Harper & Row, Publishers, 1967. 438 p.

This volume contains articles on the socioeconomic condition of minority groups, the causes of those conditions, and possible solutions.

Rutledge, Aaron L., and Gass, Gertrude Z. NINETEEN NEGRO MEN. San Francisco: Jossey-Bass, 1966. 109 p.

Rutledge and Gass chronicle the sociopsychological problems encountered in a program to retrain unemployed black men.

Ryan, William. BLAMING THE VICTIM. New York: Pantheon Books, 1971. 299 p.

Ryan contends that emphasis upon "cultural deprivation" in explaining the economic condition of the poor and racial and ethnic minorities is merely a way of avoiding the real issue of improving living standards and defers solutions to a time after cultural change has occurred. He advocates a vast redistribution of income and wealth.

Sheppard, Harold L., and Striner, Herbert E. CIVIL RIGHTS, EMPLOYMENT, AND THE SOCIAL STATUS OF AMERICAN NEGROES. Kalamazoo, Mich.: W. E. Upjohn Institute for Employment Research, June 1966. 85 p.

Sheppard and Striner examine the black economic condition and outline remedial procedures in a discussion of the interrelationship between middle-class values and income and the issue of whether one can be changed without changing the other.

Toplin, Robert B. "Reinterpreting Comparative Race Relations." JOURNAL OF BLACK STUDIES 2 (December 1971): 135-55.

Toplin disputes the contention that Brazil has more racial harmony than the United States.

Wolkon, George H. "African Identity of the Negro American and Achievement." JOURNAL OF SOCIAL ISSUES 27 (December 1971): 199-211.

Wolkon finds that black college students who identify their nationality as "American" tend to have higher grade point averages than those who designate their nationality as "African." This may result from greater adaptation to white middle-class culture.

Chapter 3

QUALITY AND ECONOMIC RETURNS
OF BLACK EDUCATION

Chapter 3

QUALITY AND ECONOMIC RETURNS
OF BLACK EDUCATION

Allen, Anne. "Taxonomy of Higher Education Barriers and Interventions for Minority and Low-Income Students." JOURNAL OF BLACK STUDIES 1 (March 1971): 357-66.

> Allen specifies the barriers to college education for blacks and lists policy interventions for both enrollment and completion in terms of sociological, economic, geographical, and psychological factors. The prime feature of this article is its comprehensive nature. Allen views the goal of improving black education as unobtainable unless a multi-faceted policy is adopted.

Baron, Harold M. "Race and Status in School Spending: Chicago, 1961-1966." JOURNAL OF HUMAN RESOURCES 6 (Winter 1971): 3-24. Tables.

> Baron observes that empirical studies have established that the race and social status of a school's student body determine expenditures on education. In Chicago during the early 1960s, expenditures were higher for whites and upper-socioeconomic class groups in both the central city and the suburbs. The pressures of the civil rights movement and new federal funds for children from low-income families had the effect of equalizing expenditures. By 1966 only schools in high-status white suburbs maintained the same degree of advantage over other groups in spending for their pupils.

Bloom, Benjamin S., et al. COMPENSATORY EDUCATION FOR CULTURAL DEPRIVATION. New York: Holt, Rinehart and Winston, 1967. 179 p.

> The authors describe the functional relationship between cultural deprivation and education. The volume contains an extensive annotated bibliography on compensatory education, which is of value to the researcher.

Brimmer, Andrew F. "The Black Revolution and the Economic Future of Negroes in the United States." AMERICAN SCHOLAR 38 (Winter 1969): 629-43. Tables.

> Brimmer chronicles a slow improvement in the relative economic condition of blacks and outlines measures for the continuation of

45

progress, including greater effort on the part of black youth to improve technical competence, acquire marketable skills, and enhance their ability to compete in an economy with expanding opportunity.

. "The Economic Outlook and the Future of the Negro College." DAEDALUS 100 (Summer 1971): 539-72.

Brimmer predicts that black colleges in general have a promising future over the next decade. Some, however, will incur serious difficulties, particularly the private institutions. The financial difficulties for both white and black private colleges are a result of rising costs and declining enrollments.

Bullough, Bonnie. "Alienation and School Segregation." INTEGRATED EDU-CATION 10 (March/April 1972): 30-35.

Bullough reports that black students residing in predominantly white suburbs and attending predominantly white schools are not as alien-ated as blacks in segregated neighborhoods and schools. It is un-clear whether this is the result of suburbanization per se or the higher income class of suburban blacks.

Carithers, Martha W. "School Desegregation and Racial Cleavage, 1954-1970: A Review of the Literature." JOURNAL OF SOCIAL ISSUES 26 (Autumn 1970): 25-47.

Carithers surveys research on the attitudinal effects of school de-segregation on whites and blacks. No general agreement or con-clusion is drawn since the evidence presented in the studies varies to such a great degree.

Chachkin, Norman J. "Metropolitan School Desegregation: Evolving Law." INTEGRATED EDUCATION 10 (March/April 1972): 13-26.

Chachkin asserts that by consolidating central city and suburban schools into metropolitan districts, racial integration and equaliza-tion of expenditures per student is more likely to occur. Recent court decisions indicate that widespread consolidation may occur in the future.

Clark, Kenneth B. "Alternative Public School Systems." HARVARD EDUCA-TIONAL REVIEW 38 (Winter 1968): 100-113.

Because of the obstacles facing integrated public schools, Clark proposes alternative forms of school control. Among the alterna-tives to local government control are schools operated by the fed-eral government and labor unions.

. "Social and Economic Implications of Integration in the Public Schools." In SEMINAR ON MANPOWER POLICY AND PROGRAMS, pp. 3-20. Washing-ton, D.C.: Manpower Administration, Office of Manpower, Automation, and

Training, 1964. Sold by Government Printing Office.

Clark testifies that the public schools do the discriminating for prejudiced employers and unions. By maintaining minimum standards in basic subjects like reading and arithmetic, the vast majority of working class black youths are unable to meet the standards for other than menial, low-paying jobs.

Cohen, David K. "Defining Racial Equality in Education." UCLA LAW REVIEW 16 (February 1969): 255-80.

Cohen asserts that desegregation will not provide equality in educational achievement, nor will equality of expenditures on education. Yet, these are the two most generally accepted standards in assessing racial equality in education. Defining equality of educational opportunity as equality in educational achievement is necessary in order to reduce economic differentials.

Coleman, James [J.]. "The Concept of Equality of Educational Opportunity." HARVARD EDUCATIONAL REVIEW 38 (Winter 1968): 7-22.

Commission on School Integration. PUBLIC SCHOOL SEGREGATION AND INTEGRATION IN THE NORTH. Washington, D.C.: National Association of Intergroup Relations Officials, 1963. 42 p. Tables.

The Commission traces the historical development of de jure and de facto school segregation in the North. It examines the quality of education in black schools and finds it to be far behind that of exclusively white schools in terms of student-teacher ratios, teacher experience, and expenditures per pupil.

Crossland, Fred E. MINORITY ACCESS TO COLLEGE. New York: Schocken, 1971. 139 p.

Crossland observes that few colleges have made firm commitments to increase minority student enrollments substantially. Therefore, low minority participation can be expected in the future unless active recruitment, remedial education, adjustment programs, and financial assistance are provided.

Dye, Thomas R. "Urban School Segregation: A Comparative Analysis." URBAN AFFAIRS QUARTERLY 4 (December 1968): 141-67. Tables.

Dye examines the influence of a number of characteristics of urban areas upon the degree of school segregation in the cities. The factors investigated are sections of the country, percentage of black enrollment in the urban area, socioeconomic class of the population, ethnic composition, size and age of the city, private school enrollment, the form of city government and type of election, method of school board selection, voter participation rates, and political party preferences.

Eder, Paula Ruth. "Deference Behavior in Play Group Situations: A Plea for Segregated Education." URBAN EDUCATION 7 (April 1972): 49-65.

Black children bused to white schools showed significant deference for whites. Eder observed that black parents did not like the system which places their children in low achievement groups in integrated schools. Racially segregated education will serve the black community better than an integrated education system which treats black students as inferiors.

Glickstein, Howard A. "Federal Educational Programs and Minority Groups." JOURNAL OF NEGRO EDUCATION 38 (Summer 1969): 303-14.

Deficiencies in federal programs to improve the education of minorities include piecemeal strategy and inadequate financing.

Gordon, Edmund W., and Jablonsky, Adelaide. "Compensatory Education in the Equalization of Educational Opportunity." JOURNAL OF NEGRO EDUCATION 37 (Summer 1968): 268-79.

Green, Robert L. "Racism in American Education." PHI DELTA KAPPAN 53 (January 1972): 274-76.

Green states that racism in education is reflected in segregated school boundaries, large numbers of teachers teaching out of their field of specialization in black schools, tracking of students, and racist teacher training institutions. Green does not provide adequate empirical evidence to support his contentions. The value of this article is the hypothesis for research which it suggests.

Gwartney, James D. "Discrimination, Achievement, and Payoffs of a College Degree." THE JOURNAL OF HUMAN RESOURCES 7 (Winter 1972): 60-70. Tables.

According to Gwartney, well qualified blacks are not relegated to low-paying, menial jobs. Employment discrimination is not most intense at the top of the job hierarchy. After adjustment for achievement, the nonwhite earnings ratio was found to be greater for college graduates than for any other educational grouping. This was true for all sex, region, and age groupings.

Hindelang, Michael James. "Educational and Occupational Aspirations among Working Class Negro, Mexican-American and White Elementary School Children." JOURNAL OF NEGRO EDUCATION 39 (Fall 1970): 351-53.

Hindelang observes that for equal educational aspirations black students had lower occupational aspirations than white and Mexican-American students--an indication that blacks may anticipate employment discrimination in the future to a greater degree than Mexican-Americans. In view of the difference in occupational attainment between blacks and whites with comparable levels of education, black anticipations reflect an accurate picture of their employment prospects.

Hines, Fred, et al. "Social and Private Rates of Return to Investment in Schooling, by Race-Sex Groups and Regions." JOURNAL OF HUMAN RESOURCES 5
(Summer 1970): 318-40. Tables.

Hines observes that private rates of return on education are high
for white and nonwhite males and females. High social rates of
return were associated in general with low levels of social investment in schooling. The South, with the lowest level of schooling
per student, incurred the highest social rate of return on educational
expenditures.

Howard, William. "Blacks and Professional Schools." CHANGE 4 (February
1972): 13-16.

Howard reports that the admission of blacks to professional schools
is growing very slowly. Developing professional schools at black
colleges is expensive with public and private sources of financial
support lacking. Reliance upon white dominated institutions appears
to be necessary.

Jones, James D., et al. "Increasing the Gap between Whites and Blacks."
EDUCATION AND URBAN SOCIETY 4 (May 1972): 339-49.

The authors report that black students are placed at an increasing
rate in lower tracks in the tracking system as they advance in
grade level. The differential in educational achievement between
blacks and whites appears to increase as grade level increases.

Marascuilo, Leonard A., and McSweeney, Maryellen. "Tracking and Minority
Student Attitudes and Performance." URBAN EDUCATION 6 (January 1972):
303-19.

Marascuilo and McSweeney find homogeneous grouping of minority
students according to ability is not necessary for attaining effective
educational performance. Where tracking results in segregated
classes, a more effective strategy would be to group classes according to heterogeneous ability.

Miller, S. M., and Roby, Pamela A. "Social Mobility, Equality, and Education." SOCIAL POLICY (May/June 1970): 38-40.

Miller and Roby contend that education has not adequately developed
labor skills nor promoted social class mobility. Students from lower
socioeconomic classes are not enabled to compete with those from
higher classes. Equal opportunity will be more likely assured when
present patterns of hiring and promotion are not so largely predicated
on educational attainment.

Mommsen, Kent G. "Professionalism and the Racial Context of Career Patterns
among Black American Doctorates: A Note on the Brain Drain Hypothesis."
JOURNAL OF NEGRO EDUCATION 42 (Spring 1973): 191-204.

A survey by Mommsen indicates that black colleges are unable to

acquire or retain an increasing proportion of black academicians.
An external cost resulting from federal government efforts to increase black faculty at white dominated colleges is to leave the
black colleges with their poor financial resources and without many
of their best faculty. A potential solution is to increase black
graduate school enrollments.

Nam, Charles B., et al. "School Retention by Race, Religion, and Socioeconomic Status." JOURNAL OF HUMAN RESOURCES 3 (Spring 1968): 171-90.
Tables.

The authors report that low socioeconomic level, non-Catholic religious identification, and residence in the South are more closely associated than race with leaving school before graduation. Blue-collar
blacks in urbanized areas of the North and West and blue-collar white
males in rural parts of the South have the highest dropout rates.

Nelson, William C. "The Storefront School: A Vehicle for Change." JOUR-
NAL OF NEGRO EDUCATION 40 (Summer 1971): 248-54.

Nelson examines an alternative form of education for reaching
disadvantaged urban black youth.

Perry, Jane Greverus. "The Job Outlook for Negro Youth." JOURNAL OF
NEGRO EDUCATION 33 (Spring 1964): 111-16.

Perry examines the employment condition of black youth and finds
it to be abysmal. Among the major obstacles are confinement to
declining industries and a lack of training for expanding occupations.

Pettigrew, Thomas F. "Negro American Intelligence: A New Look at an Old
Controversy." In BASIC EDUCATION FOR THE DISADVANTAGED ADULT,
pp. 111-33. Edited by Frank W. Lanning and Wesley A. Many. Boston:
Houghton Mifflin Co., 1966.

Pettigrew examines research on the reasons why blacks generally
score lower on intelligence tests than whites. While genetic
explanations do not bear up under scrutiny, environmental influences are not neutral factors in intelligence tests.

. "Race and Equal Educational Opportunity." HARVARD EDUCATIONAL
REVIEW 38 (Winter 1968): 66-76.

. "Racial Segregation and Negro Education." In TOWARD A NATIONAL
URBAN POLICY, pp. 167-77. Edited by Daniel P. Moynihan. New York:
Basic Books, 1970.

Pettigrew describes the increasing rate of segregation in northern
urban schools and the failure of the schools to achieve educational
equality. He recommends metropolitan school districts in order to
equalize expenditures per student and to promote integration.

Puryear, Mahlon T. "Technology and the Negro." In NEGROES AND JOBS, pp. 197-212. Edited by Louis A. Ferman et al. Ann Arbor: University of Michigan Press, 1968.

Of unemployed blacks, Puryear estimates that 70 percent are not academically prepared to master short-term retraining programs. The assumption is false that the untrained want to be trained.

Raymond, Richard. "Regional Differences in Racial Discrimination in Education and Employment." WESTERN ECONOMIC JOURNAL 8 (June 1970): 190-208.

Raymond observes that discrimination in education appears to be more prevalent in the South than in the non-South, although lower revenue sources for education in the South is a partial explanation. Employment discrimination in the South and restriction of blacks from higher-paying, higher-status occupations in the non-South exist. Economic growth has little favorable impact on nonwhites due to labor market rigidities in both regions. Raymond encounters difficulties in his analysis of the correlation between occupational mobility and economic growth by failing to account for the fact that economic growth in a geographical area also tends to increase the supply of available labor as employers tap other labor markets. A condition of long-term, sustained national growth might reduce occupational rigidities for nonwhites.

Rees, Helen E. DEPRIVATION AND COMPENSATORY EDUCATION. Boston: Houghton Mifflin Co., 1968. 300 p. Tables.

Rempson, Joseph L. "Minority Access to Higher Education in New York City." CITY ALMANAC 7 (August 1972): 1-15.

Rempson observes that the policy of open enrollment to colleges operated by the City of New York has substantially increased the participation of blacks and Puerto Ricans. Whites with low school achievement records, however, are prime beneficiaries.

Ribich, Thomas S. "The Problem of Equal Opportunity: A Review Article." JOURNAL OF HUMAN RESOURCES 7 (Fall 1972): 518-26.

Ribich examines the issue of equalizing per-student educational expenditures. Providing equal educational opportunity is only one small step toward equalizing the chances of the poor to climb into upper socioeconomic ranks. Equalizing educational expenditures per pupil between black and white students may have little effect upon incomes.

Rodgers, Harrel R., Jr., and Bullock, Charles S. III. "School Desegregation-- A Policy Analysis." JOURNAL OF BLACK STUDIES 2 (June 1972): 409-38. Tables.

Rodgers and Bullock observe that desegregation has proceeded slowly due to a lack of federal government support. Segregated

schools retard the achievement of black students and will only be
eliminated through concerted federal policy.

St. John, Nancy, and Lewis, Ralph. "The Influence of School Racial Context
on Academic Achievement." SOCIAL PROBLEMS 19 (Summer 1971): 68-78.
Tables.

St. John and Lewis found that both black and white sixth grade
students achieve at higher levels in schools over 50 percent white.
Other factors, which might account for the differential in achievement, such as family income and attitudes of parents toward education, are not considered.

Sexton, Patricia Cayo. "City Schools." In NEGROES AND JOBS, pp. 222-
36. Edited by Louis A. Ferman et al. Ann Arbor: University of Michigan
Press, 1968.

Sexton chronicles the inequality between predominantly black and
white schools in the City of Detroit on the basis of expenditures
per pupil, class size, teacher experience, and age of physical
plant. Quality of education is a function of income class, which
is a function of race.

_____. EDUCATION AND INCOME; INEQUALITIES OF OPPORTUNITY IN
OUR PUBLIC SCHOOLS. New York: Viking Press, 1961. 298 p. Tables.

Sexton demonstrates an inverse correlation between the quality of
education provided and the income of residents of the City of
Detroit.

Shanks, Hershel. "Equal Education and the Law." AMERICAN SCHOLAR 39
(Spring 1970): 255-69.

Shanks observes that the law does not require states to equalize
per-pupil expenditures on education. Educational inequality is,
therefore, perpetuated. However, the author's basic assumption
that a direct correlation exists between educational expenditures
and educational quality is not wholly supported by empirical
evidence.

Smith, Barbara Lee, and Hughes, Anita L. " 'Spillover' Effect of the Black
Educated." JOURNAL OF BLACK STUDIES 4 (September 1973): 52-68.

Smith and Hughes propose greater interdependence between black
colleges and black communities so as to take advantage of the
benefits each provides to the other.

Smith, John W., and Smith, Betty M. "For Black Educators: Integration
Brings the Axe." URBAN REVIEW 6 (1973): 7-12.

The Smiths chronicle the displacement of black teachers in the
South as a result of school integration. The integration of student

Chapter 4

BLACK MOVEMENT TO
AND WITHIN URBAN AREAS

Chapter 4

BLACK MOVEMENT TO AND WITHIN URBAN AREAS

Adams, E. Sherman. "Coping with Ghetto Unemployment." CONFERENCE
BOARD RECORD 7 (May 1970): 41-45.

> Adams states that the movement of industry to the suburbs results
> in high ghetto unemployment. He recommends that jobs be created
> in ghetto areas and ghetto workers be given access to suburban job
> markets via transportation and housing availability. Reasons for
> the movement of industry to the suburbs are the scarcity of inner
> city sites, high land costs, and high taxes. Public subsidies could
> reduce these private costs.

Baughman, E. Earl, and Dahlstrom, W. Grant. NEGRO AND WHITE CHIL-
DREN: A PSYCHOLOGICAL STUDY IN THE RURAL SOUTH. New York:
Academic Press, 1968. 572 p.

> Baughman and Dahlstrom focus upon a rural poverty area where
> blacks are a majority of the population, but where whites control
> the political and economic systems. Migration of black youth out
> of the area is high and forced by conditions in the area. Black
> migration is motivated in a large part by escape from socioeconomic
> conditions in the rural South.

Bernstein, Samuel J. "Mass Transit and the Urban Ghetto." TRAFFIC QUAR-
TERLY 27 (July 1973): 431-49.

> Bernstein surveys blacks and Puerto Ricans in New York City as to
> the services they desire from the urban transportation system. Mass
> transportation access to suburban employment markets does not appear
> to be a major concern.

Burtt, Everett J., Jr. PLANT RELOCATION AND THE CORE CITY WORKER.
Washington, D.C.: U.S. Government Printing Office, 1967. 166 p. Tables.

> Burt examines the effects on core city residents of plants being relocated
> from central city Boston to the suburbs. For those core city residents
> remaining with the firms, actual out-of-pocket costs for travel and
> time lost through commuting were significant. Many workers did
> not remain with the firms due to the increased costs.

Elgie, Robert. "Rural Immigration, Urban Ghettoization, and Their Consequences." ANTIPODE: A RADICAL JOURNAL OF GEOGRAPHY 2 (December 1970): 35-54.

> According to Elgie, guaranteed annual income plans will not sub-stantially improve the condition of the urban black poor as long as the urban spatial structure perpetuates ghettoization and its conse-quent inequality in employment and education. A major difficulty with the article is the author's failure to adequately distinguish between relative and absolute poverty. Guaranteed annual income plans depending, of course, upon the level of benefits should elim-inate absolute poverty--at least as defined by the U.S. Department of Labor.

Fusfeld, Daniel R. "The Basic Economics of the Urban and Racial Crisis." In CONFERENCE PAPERS OF THE UNION FOR RADICAL POLITICAL ECONOM-ICS, pp. 55-84. Ann Arbor, Mich.: The Union for Radical Political Eco-nomics, 1968.

> Fusfeld largely attributes the impoverished socioeconomic condition of blacks to their migration to central cities at a time which cor-responds with a period of declining demand for unskilled labor. At the same time, the economic base of central cities is declining, which accounts for the deteriorating supply of public services offered by the cities. For further development of this topic see Fusfeld's THE BASIC ECONOMICS OF THE URBAN RACIAL CRISIS in Chapter 4.

Goering, John M., and Kalachek, Edward M. "Public Transportation and Black Unemployment." SOCIETY 10 (July/August 1973): 39-42.

> Goering and Kalachek report that an experiment in St. Louis to provide bus transportation for black inner city residents to suburban employment areas failed. Providing automobiles to each rider would have been cheaper. Small numbers of blacks secured employment in suburban areas as a result of the transportation program.

Grindstaff, C.F. "The Negro, Urbanization, and Relative Deprivation in the Deep South." SOCIAL PROBLEMS 15 (September 1968): 342-52. Tables.

> According to Grindstaff, the economic difference between blacks and whites widens as blacks move from the deep South to urban areas. In absolute terms, however, blacks appear to be better off economically in urban areas than in the rural South.

Hauser, Philip M. "Demographic and Social Factors in the Poverty of the Negro." In THE DISADVANTAGED POOR: EDUCATION AND EMPLOYMENT, pp. 229-61. By Task Force on Economic Growth and Opportunity. Washington, D.C.: Chamber of Commerce of the United States, 1966.

> Hauser traces the demographic changes experienced by blacks since the Civil War. He compares the condition of blacks with that of white immigrants and concludes that the primary factors retarding black economic progress are white prejudice and high birth rates.

Hilaski, Harvey J. "How Poverty Area Residents Look for Work." MONTHLY LABOR REVIEW (March 1971): 41-45.

Hilaski finds that information provided by relatives is the most effective means for poverty area residents to find out about job openings. The methods of eliciting job market information do not appreciably differ between the poor and nonpoor. The nonpoor have greater access to information about higher paying job opportunities than the poor.

Jenkins, Mercilee M. "Age and Migration Factors in the Socioeconomic Conditions of Urban Black and Urban White Women." INDUSTRIAL GERONTOLOGY 9 (Spring 1971): 13-17.

Jenkins finds that urban black women experience more part-time and seasonal employment than their white counterparts. Migrants to urban areas do not appear to be less educated or experience greater unemployment than nonmigrants. Migration does not appear to worsen and in many instances improves the economic condition of black migrants.

Kain, John F. "The Big Cities' Big Problem." In NEGROES AND JOBS, pp. 236-44. Edited by Louis A. Ferman et al. Ann Arbor: University of Michigan Press, 1968. Tables.

Kain observes that housing segregation coupled with inadequate transportation systems severely limit the employment of ghetto blacks, and estimates the number of jobs lost in Chicago and Detroit due to these factors. Suburbanization of blacks is the only long-run solution to the urban problems stemming from housing segregation.

_____. "Housing Segregation, Negro Employment, and Metropolitan Decentralization." QUARTERLY JOURNAL OF ECONOMICS 82 (May 1968): 175-97. Tables.

Kain finds that racial segregation in metropolitan housing markets reduces the employment opportunities of blacks. The growing postwar suburbanization of metropolitan employment further undermines the position of the black worker. According to Kain, continued high levels of black unemployment in a full employment economy may be attributable to the rapid and adverse shifts in the location of jobs.

Kaun, David E. "Negro Migration and Unemployment." HUMAN RESOURCES 5 (Spring 1970): 191-207.

Kaun finds that the areas into which blacks migrate from the South bear a positive relationship to regional income differentials but not to differences in the unemployment rate. A problem with this study is that it does not account for investment in human capital differentials in terms of education and training.

Kidder, Alice [E.] Handsaker. "Job Search Among Negroes." LABOR LAW JOUR-
NAL 19 (August 1968): 482-88.

> Kidder reports that blacks tend to restrict their job search to tradi-
> tional black jobs and experience higher rejection rates than whites
> when applying for integrated jobs. She recommends both a tax on
> employers who do not actively recruit blacks and subsidized transpor-
> tation from the central city to industrial suburbs for black workers.

_____. "Racial Differences in Job Search and Wages." MONTHLY LABOR
REVIEW 91 (July 1968): 24-26.

> Kidder reports that black workers search more intensively for jobs
> and suffer higher rejection rates than their white counterparts.
> The majority of blacks confine their search to jobs which they have
> traditionally held. Blacks utilize the state employment services
> more frequently than whites, who rely upon informal sources for
> job market information more than upon formal sources. The opposite
> is true for blacks, and those seeking nontraditional jobs encounter
> discrimination.

Lurie, Melvin, and Rayack, Elton. "Employment Opportunities for Negro
Families in Satellite Cities." SOUTHERN ECONOMIC JOURNAL 36 (October
1969): 191-95.

> Lurie and Rayack examine the employment of blacks in small cities
> and conclude that greater opportunity for advancement exists there
> than in large central cities. Redistribution of the black population
> to smaller cities is encouraged.

_____. "Racial Differences in Migration and Job Search: A Case Study."
In NEGROES AND JOBS, pp. 358-82. Edited by Louis A. Ferman et al.
Ann Arbor: University of Michigan Press, 1968. Tables.

> Lurie and Rayack surveyed the techniques utilized by blacks and
> whites to locate jobs in a small town. While both blacks and
> whites relied upon informal sources of information--friends and
> relatives, and direct applications--rather than formal sources--
> state and private employment services, want ads, and unions--
> blacks relied more heavily on the state service and less on private
> employment services.

Masters, Stanley H. "Are Black Migrants from the South to the Northern Cities
Worse Off than Blacks Already There?" JOURNAL OF HUMAN RESOURCES
7 (Fall 1972): 411-23. Tables.

> With or without standardizing for differences in age, years of
> school, and a number of other variables, Masters finds that among
> blacks living in metropolitan areas outside the South in 1960, those
> born in the South had higher incomes and less unemployment than
> those born in the North. Although the differential is larger for
> whites than for blacks, recent migrants, defined as those living in
> a metropolitan area in 1960 but not in 1955, did have lower in-

comes than those who were in metropolitan areas in both years.

Michelson, Stephan. "Rational Income Decisions of Negroes and Everyone Else." INDUSTRIAL AND LABOR RELATIONS REVIEW 23 (October 1969): 15-28. Tables.

Michelson speculates that presumably career choices are made in a manner which will maximize income. But an individual's perception of what income will be and actual income differ widely. Black migrants to the North are often motivated by an expectation of high income with little awareness of the probability of achieving it. Southern blacks have a great incentive to move North, and all blacks have a great incentive to continue their education. This indicates more black schooling, migration, and in the absence of reward for those accomplishments, greater frustration.

Mooney, Joseph D. "Housing Segregation, Negro Employment and Metropolitan Decentralization: An Alternative Perspective." QUARTERLY JOURNAL OF ECONOMICS 83 (May 1969): 299-311. Tables.

Mooney finds that the dispersal of industry from central cities to the suburbs reduces the employment opportunities for blacks living in segregated inner city neighborhoods. The maintenance of high aggregate demand, however, may have a more beneficial effect than efforts to improve transportation between the inner city and the suburbs.

Mueller, Eva, and Ladd, William. "Negro-White Differences in Geographic Mobility." In NEGROES AND JOBS, pp. 382-400. Edited by Louis A. Ferman et al. Ann Arbor: University of Michigan Press, 1968. Tables.

Mueller and Ladd contrast the rate and geographic pattern of mobility between blacks and whites. Black families are less mobile than white families. Family ties to a place or uneasiness about unfamiliar surroundings are barriers to mobility among blacks primarily when economic incentives to move are weak. Although unemployment does not create an incentive for either blacks or whites to move, mobility among blacks with low levels of education is less.

Niedercorn, J. H. SUBURBANIZATION OF EMPLOYMENT AND POPULATION. New York: Rand Corp., 1963. 381 p.

Niedercorn chronicles the movement of white residents and jobs to the suburbs, away from the central cities where blacks reside.

O'Kane, James M. "Ethnic Mobility and the Lower-Income Negro: A Socio-Historical Perspective." SOCIAL PROBLEMS 16 (Winter 1969): 302-11.

O'Kane contends that the routes to economic advancement followed by earlier migrant groups to the cities are closed to blacks. Government sponsored programs designed to improve the economic con-

dition of blacks do not adequately account for the changing structure of the labor market away from unskilled jobs to skilled occupations.

Persky, Joseph J., and Kain, John F. "Migration, Employment, and Race in
the Deep South." SOUTHERN ECONOMIC QUARTERLY 36 (January 1970):
268-76.

Employment discrimination and black migration is highest from
southern rural areas with high black-white population ratios.
Black migration to crowded metropolitan areas would be reduced
through economic development and a reduction of racial discrimination in these areas, and perhaps would be more advantageous to
blacks than migration from the South.

Raymond, Richard. "Determinants of Non-White Migration During the 1950s:
Their Regional Significance and Long-Run Implications." AMERICAN JOURNAL
OF ECONOMICS AND SOCIOLOGY 31 (January 1972): 9-20. Tables.

Raymond observes that during the 1950s nonwhites moved away from
regions of the country where their economic status was poor and
toward areas in which their condition was somewhat better. If
nonwhites respond consistently to economic stimuli in this manner,
then their migration patterns will tend to improve their economic
status as a group. Since one cannot always rely upon economic
forces, Raymond recommends a concentrated program of information
dissemination and migration subsidies.

_____. "Mobility and Economic Progress of Negro Americans during the
1940s." AMERICAN JOURNAL OF ECONOMICS AND SOCIOLOGY 28
(October 1969): 337-50. Tables.

Measured in absolute terms, the economic condition of blacks improved during the 1940s. A significant portion of the improvement
is attributable to upward occupational mobility. Rural to urban
migration was relatively unimportant.

Read, Peter B. "Migration and Mobility: The Myth of a Northern Haven for
Blacks." CORNELL JOURNAL OF SOCIAL RELATIONS 5 (Spring 1970): 57-
76.

According to Read, migration to the North has not improved the
socioeconomic condition of blacks appreciably due to discrimination in housing, education, and employment. Read fails to examine
other determinants of socioeconomic conditions such as access to
political machinery and public accommodations.

Stevens, David W. SUPPLEMENTAL LABOR MARKET INFORMATION AS A
MEANS TO INCREASE THE EFFECTIVENESS OF JOB-SEARCH ACTIVITY. Uni-
versity Park: Institute for Research on Human Resources, Pennsylvania State
University Press, 1968. 166 p. Tables.

Stevens analyzes the effects of a program to provide increased
labor market information to unemployed whites and blacks. Among
blacks the increased information significantly improved employment,
while among whites it had little effect.

Stevenson, Gloria. "Channels to Opportunity." MANPOWER 2 (April 1970):
2-8.

Stevenson describes the operation of a Chicago television program
designed to provide information on job opportunities to the unemployed. The state employment service is the major contributor of
job market information. However, employers not normally utilizing
state employment services do not appear to be listing job opportunities on the television program.

Taylor, William L. "The Immigrant Myth." In HANGING TOGETHER, pp.
48-82. New York: Simon and Schuster, 1970.

Taylor compares the situation of previous immigrants with that of
black migrants. He finds the former to have had distinct advantages due to the demand for unskilled labor. This demand has been
declining as a proportion of the total labor market demand since
World War II, the period of greatest black migration.

Tilly, Charles. "Migration to American Cities." In TOWARD A NATIONAL
URBAN POLICY, pp. 152-66. Edited by Daniel P. Moynihan. New York:
Basic Books, 1970.

Tilly contends that black migrants to the cities have not achieved
the economic success of other migrant groups because of discrimination. An interesting analysis which the author does not undertake
is a comparison of educational attainment and labor market skills
for white immigrants and black migrants upon arrival. Labor market
demand in terms of both its composition and its total could be compared during the periods of greatest immigration and migration.

. "Race and Migration to the American City." In THE METROPOLITAN
ENIGMA: INQUIRIES INTO THE NATURE AND DIMENSIONS OF AMERICA'S
'URBAN CRISIS'," pp. 124-46. Edited by James L. Wilson. Washington, D.C.:
U.S. Chamber of Commerce, 1967.

Tilly observes that job opportunities are the prime determinant of
the rate of black migration from rural to urban areas. He contends
that the problems confronting black migrants and the disruption of
urban areas caused by migrants are greatly exaggerated. Never-
theless, Tilly advocates public policies to ease the transition.

United States Department of Commerce. NEGRO-WHITE DIFFERENCES IN
GEOGRAPHIC MOBILITY. Washington, D.C.: 1964. 22 p. Sold by Government Printing Office.

This report discloses that geographical mobility for blacks is appreciably less than for whites.

Walls, Dwayne. THE CHICKENBONE SPECIAL. Atlanta, Ga.: Southern Regional Council, 1970. 44 p.

Walls describes the socioeconomic conditions which motivate black migration from the South to the North and the period of transition in the North for black migrants.

Walton, Sidney. "Geographic Proposals for Black Economic Liberation." BLACK SCHOLAR 3 (February 1972): 38-48.

Black migration is mainly to urban areas already experiencing high black unemployment because information about economic opportunities in other geographical areas is lacking. Walton proposes a national economic integration program to initiate outmigration of blacks from urban areas with high unemployment to areas with shortages of labor.

Wheeler, James O. "Work Trip Length and the Ghetto." LAND ECONOMICS 44 (February 1968): 107-12. Tables.

Wheeler finds that the travel distance from home to place of employment is greater for ghetto residents than nonghetto residents.

Chapter 5

BLACKS IN RESIDENTIAL HOUSING MARKETS

Chapter 5

BLACKS IN RESIDENTIAL HOUSING MARKETS

Alston, Jon P. "The Black Population in Urbanized Areas, 1960." JOURNAL OF BLACK STUDIES 1 (June 1971): 435-42. Tables.

Alston finds that the suburbs contain blacks with higher socioeconomic standings than the central cities. The suburbs also contain some blacks who are not middle class, but they comprise a small proportion of the total.

Baum, Daniel J. TOWARD A FREE HOUSING MARKET. Coral Gables, Fla.: University of Miami Press, 1971. 241 p.

Baum examines federal government policies which have promoted housing segregation and describes a Federal Housing Administration program designed to promote integration.

Bonham, Gordon Scott. "Discrimination and Housing Quality." GROWTH AND CHANGE 3 (October 1972): 26-34. Tables.

Bonham observes that nonwhites occupy poorer quality housing than whites even when both groups have other similar socioeconomic characteristics. By controlling differences between white and nonwhite households, there remains a difference in housing quality which can be considered a quantitative measure of discrimination in renter occupied housing.

Boston, John, et al. "The Impact of Race on Housing Markets." SOCIAL PROBLEMS 19 (Winter 1972): 382-93.

The authors review the literature on race and property values with special attention to problems of measurement and analysis. Strategies in gathering and validating selling price data and standardizing prices for "real value" are reviewed. The article provides valuable information on research methodologies for those interested in adding to the literature on the effects of racial integration on property values.

Bradford, David F., and Kelejian, Harry H. "An Econometric Model of the Flight to the Suburbs." JOURNAL OF POLITICAL ECONOMY 81 (May/June

1973): 566-89. Tables.

> Bradford and Kelejian find that the residential location decisions of middle and upper-income class families are determined by the rent differential between the city and suburbs and by the location of poor families. The racial composition of the central city does not appear to affect the residential location decision between central cities and suburbs for either middle-class or poor whites.

Carbine, Michael E. "Rebuilding the Ghetto from Within." MANPOWER 2 (June 1970): 7-10.

> Carbine examines a project in Washington, D.C., whereby black construction workers rehabilitate existing dwellings. He finds this approach to be a potentially cheaper method of providing adequate housing than publicly financed new construction.

Christensen, Edward A. "The Public Housing Leasing Program: A Workable Rent Subsidy?" URBAN LAW ANNUAL (1968): 57-75.

> Christensen evaluates the effects of the public housing leasing program upon the quality of housing available to the poor and residential segregation patterns. He concludes that it is a better program than direct rent subsidization.

Connolly, Harold X. "Black Movement into the Suburbs: Suburbs Doubling Their Black Populations during the 1960s." URBAN AFFAIRS QUARTERLY 9 (September 1973): 91-111.

> The increased movement of blacks into suburban areas has not substantially increased the degree of integrated housing. Only a small proportion of the black population is represented, and some suburban communities are almost exclusively black.

Davidoff, Paul, and Gold, Neil N. "Exclusionary Zoning." LAW AND SOCIAL ACTION 1 (Winter 1970): 56-63.

> Davidoff and Gold propose state government action to combat municipal zoning ordinances which perpetuate racial and class segregation. Restrictions on lot size and cost per dwelling, and multi-family units reduce the likelihood of racial integration.

Deutsch, Martin, and Collins, Mary E. INTERRACIAL HOUSING: A PSYCHO-LOGICAL EVALUATION OF A SOCIAL EXPERIMENT. Minneapolis: University of Minnesota Press, 1968. 173 p.

Fielding, Byron. "Home Ownership for Low Income Families." JOURNAL OF HOUSING 6 (June 1969): 278-79.

> Fielding traces the development of federal subsidization of housing. Only in recent years have low-income consumers received much benefit from federal policy, and even then the programs have been limited in scope.

Freeman, Linton C., and Sunshine, Morris. PATTERNS OF RESIDENTIAL SEG-
REGATION. Cambridge, Mass.: Schenkman Publishing Co., 1969.

Friedman, Lawrence M. GOVERNMENT AND SLUM HOUSING: A CENTURY
OF FRUSTRATION. Chicago: Rand McNally & Co., 1968. 206 p. Tables.

Friedman traces the development of governmental policy toward
slum housing. He evaluates the punitive approach and subsidization and concludes that the latter is a more effective means for
improving the housing of the poor than the traditional mode of
threatening punitive action against slum landlords.

Grier, George W. "The Negro and Federal Housing Policy." LAW AND
CONTEMPORARY PROBLEMS 32 (Summer 1967): 550-60.

Grier finds that the existence of racial ghettos is the result of
government housing policy. He advocates stricter enforcement of
antidiscrimination laws, subsidies to socioeconomically mixed housing developments, and rent and mortgage subsidies to low-income
groups. In consonance with other researchers, Grier finds that the
quality of housing for the poor can be improved more cheaply by
income supplements than by the construction of new public housing.

Grier, George W., and Grier, Eunice. EQUALITY AND BEYOND: HOUS-
ING, SEGREGATION AND THE GOALS OF THE GREAT SOCIETY. Chicago:
Quadrangle, 1969. 115 p.

Hartman, Chester W. "The Politics of Housing." DISSENT 14 (November/
December 1967): 701-14.

Hartman proposes rent subsidies as a means of allowing the filtering
process to promote racial housing integration. Other proposals are
low-interest loans and granting public housing authorities control
over entire metropolitan areas so as to prevent the reduced possibil-
ities for housing integration due to the flight of whites from central
cities to the suburbs.

Hendon, W. S. "Discrimination against Negro Homeowners in Property Tax
Assessment." AMERICAN JOURNAL OF ECONOMICS AND SOCIOLOGY
27 (1968): 125-32. Tables.

Hendon compares sale prices and property tax assessments of black
and white homes in Fort Worth, Texas. Blacks pay higher taxes
per comparable dwelling unit than do whites.

Industrial Union Department, AFL-CIO. "De Facto is for Real." IUD AGENDA
1 (July 1965): 9-11.

The report proposes the achievement of socioeconomic integration
of blacks through locating high schools in districts serving both races
and through rent supplements to enable blacks to live in white
neighborhoods. A difficulty with the former proposal is the instability

71

of racial composition of neighborhoods within central cities. A
high school built in an integrated neighborhood may soon be serving
a racially segregated student body.

Kain, John F., and Quigley, John M. "Housing Market Discrimination, Homeownership, and Savings Behavior." AMERICAN ECONOMIC REVIEW 62 (June
1972): 263-77. Tables.

Kain and Quigley find that blacks may pay from 5 to 10 percent
more than whites in most urban areas for comparable housing. Discrimination also affects the type of housing blacks select, while
home ownership is reduced among blacks because of higher prices.
A problem with this study is that it does not provide an adequate
comparison of housing quality per dollar between blacks and whites.

King, A. Thomas, and Mieszkowski, Peter. "Racial Discrimination, Segregation, and the Price of Housing." JOURNAL OF POLITICAL ECONOMY 81
(May/June 1973): 590-606. Tables.

Based upon a sample of 200 rental units with comprehensive information on the characteristics of the dwellings, it is estimated that
blacks and whites do pay different amounts for equivalent units.
For black female-headed households, the markup relative to white
males is 16 percent; for black male-headed households, 7.5 percent. King and Mieszkowski calculate that rents for whites in
integrated areas are about 7 percent lower than for black households.

Lapham, Victoria. "Do Blacks Pay More for Housing?" JOURNAL OF POLIT-
ICAL ECONOMY 79 (November/December 1971): 1244-57. Tables.

Lapham reports on the prices paid by blacks and whites for housing
in Dallas, Texas, in 1960. The price of housing was compared with
different characteristics of the houses (fireplace, garage, etc.) for
both groups. The conclusion was that no significant difference
existed between the prices blacks and whites paid for comparable
dwelling units. The study is of particular interest because of the
extent to which an attempt is made to measure housing quality.
A usual method is to use degrees of substandard housing according
to U.S. Department of Census definitions, which leaves wide latitude in making quality comparisons.

Lindeman, Bruce. "The Future of Low Priced Housing in Atlanta." ATLANTA
ECONOMIC REVIEW 21 (April 1971): 22-25.

Lindeman forecasts the requirements of government subsidy programs
in order to increase the supply of housing for low-income families
in Atlanta, Georgia. A difficulty with this study is its failure to
forecast adequately the effect of the filtering process. As higher-
income families acquire new dwellings in outlying suburbs and sell
their former dwellings to low-income families, the supply of housing
available to low-income families increases.

Low-Income Housing Demonstration Staff, Office of Program Policy Housing and Home Finance Agency. LOW-INCOME HOUSING DEMONSTRATION, A SEARCH FOR SOLUTIONS. Washington, D.C.: October 1964. Sold by Government Printing Office.

> The report examines twenty-one low-income housing demonstration projects. The researcher is provided with the opportunity of comparing his ideas on possible solutions with actual experience in the area.

Lowry, Ira S. HOUSING ASSISTANCE FOR LOW-INCOME URBAN FAMILIES. New York: Rand Institute, 1971. 57 p.

> Lowry proposes governmental policies which allow low-income families to afford well-maintained older homes which are cheaper to acquire and maintain than new residences built on reclaimed land. The filtering process would also assure better quality for the price than subsidized public housing.

McAllister, Ronald J. NEIGHBORHOOD INTEGRATION AND PROSPECTIVE RESIDENTIAL MOBILITY. Chapel Hill, N.C.: Distributed by Center for Urban and Regional Studies, 1970. 149 p.

Manvel, Allen D. HOUSING CONDITIONS IN URBAN POVERTY AREAS. Washington, D.C.: National Commission on Urban Problems, 1968. 21 p. Tables. Sold by Government Printing Office.

> Manvel compares housing in low-income areas with that in high-income areas. Vast contrasts in housing density, concentration of nonwhites, and owner occupancy exist between the two income areas.

Margolis, Richard. "Last Chance for Desegregation." DISSENT 19 (Winter 1972): 249-56.

> Margolis views segregated housing markets as primarily the result of class exploitation. A coalition of blacks and poor whites might effectively challenge class segregation.

Montgomery, Roger. "Notes on Instant Urban Renewal--Income Supplements: A New Approach to the Slum Housing Problem." TRANS-ACTION 4 (September 1967): 9-12.

> Income supplements are the most efficient means for the renovation of existing slum dwellings and the movement of slum dwellers into better-quality housing.

Nassau County Commission on Human Rights. "Causes of Racial Tension in an Urban Renewal Program." INTERRACIAL REVIEW 39 (May 1966): 105-10; 39 (June 1966): 115-22.

> Among the potential sources of racial tension resulting from urban renewal projects is the displacement of housing in black neighbor-

hoods by dwellings which the former residents of the neighborhood cannot afford.

National Committee Against Discrimination in Housing. JOBS AND HOUSING: INTERIM REPORT. New York: 1970. 250 p. Tables.

The Committee examines employment opportunities in New York City suburbs, obstacles to improved employment for blacks and Puerto Ricans in the suburbs, and means for overcoming those obstacles. Transportation from the ghetto to the suburbs offers little. Relocation of minorities in suburbs is necessary and will require a restructuring of zoning laws and housing finance methods. The conclusion that a restructured transportation system will fail to improve employment opportunities for inner city residents is well documented. However, the improvement of employment opportunities by restructuring housing markets cannot be supported or denied empirically.

Northwood, Lawrence K., and Barth, Ernest A. URBAN DESEGREGATION: NEGRO PIONEERS AND THEIR WHITE NEIGHBORS. Seattle: University of Washington Press, 1965. 131 p.

Northwood and Barth examine the effects of residential integration on both white and black families.

Norton, Eleanor Holmes. "The Most Irresponsible Industry in New York City." INTEGRATED EDUCATION 10 (March/April 1972): 8-12.

Norton criticizes the real estate industry for neglecting the welfare of minority groups in New York City.

Piven, Frances F., and Cloward R[ichard] A. "Desegregated Housing: Who Pays for the Reformer's Ideal?" THE NEW REPUBLIC 155 (December 17, 1966): 17-22.

Piven describes urban housing policies as they relate to blacks and concludes that they work at cross purposes and defeat their intention of achieving racially integrated housing. Subsidization and incentive schemes are as costly as the construction of public housing in white neighborhoods.

"Public Housing and Integration: A Neglected Opportunity." COLUMBIA JOURNAL OF LAW AND SOCIAL PROBLEMS 6 (May 1970): 253-79.

The article examines the influence of federal government policy, white opposition, and local government policy on the maintenance of segregated public housing. Because public housing is often located upon land cleared of dwellings formerly occupied by blacks, the expansion of the black population into white residential areas is retarded, while appearing to be to their best advantage. Location of public housing projects in or near white residential areas encounters the greatest resistance.

Rainwater, Lee. BEHIND GHETTO WALLS. Chicago: Aldine Publishing Co., 1970. 446 p.

Rainwater describes living conditions in a housing project sponsored by the federal government and effects of this environment on the lives of the black residents. The federal housing policy of building high-rise public projects reduces the movement of blacks into white neighborhoods. The concentration of lower socioeconomic class people in limited space often results in abnormally high crime rates and eventual abandonment of the projects.

Roof, W. Clark. "Residential Segregation of Blacks and Racial Inequality in Southern Cities: Toward a Causal Model." SOCIAL PROBLEMS 19 (Winter 1972): 393-407.

Roof examines the relation between nonwhite residential segregation and black-white differentials in education, occupation, and income for southern cities. The degree of segregation adversely affects socioeconomic variables. A difficulty with this study is that residential segregation may in fact be the effect of low income, education, and occupational standing rather than the cause.

Rose, Harold. "The All Black Town: Suburban Prototype or Rural Slum." In PEOPLE AND POLITICS IN URBAN SOCIETY, pp. 397-431. Edited by Harlan Hahn. Beverly Hills, Calif.: Sage Publications, 1972.

Rose finds that the movement of blacks into the suburbs is largely a result of spillover from adjacent ghettos. Movement away from ghettos and adjacent areas offers better education and employment opportunities, but public construction of low- and moderate-income housing in these areas has not received sufficient support. Whether the desired results in education and employment would occur as a result of black suburbanization is questionable in view of other research in this area.

Ross, Myron H. "Prices, Segregation, and Racial Harmony." JOURNAL OF BLACK STUDIES 2 (December 1971): 225. Tables.

Ross finds that the federal government has increased the extent of residential segregation and the external diseconomy that results. Governmental efforts to command desegregation via open housing laws is likely to fail or have a negligible impact. He proposes a subsidy via either property tax abatements, direct payments, lower mortgage rates, or improving public services in order to encourage integrated neighborhoods. A primary impact of residential segregation is upon black employment opportunities.

Sanoff, Henry, and Ellinwood, George. "Changing Residential Racial Patterns." URBAN AND SOCIAL CHANGE REVIEW 4 (Spring 1971): 68-71.

According to Sanoff and Ellinwood, movement of blacks into white neighborhoods does not cause property values to decline except in cases of panic selling. This is one of many studies dealing with

the effects that racial integration of neighborhoods have on property
values. All studies in this field agree that property values may fall
in the short run due to panic selling by whites. In the long run,
however, prices seem to stabilize at a level approximate to those
prior to integration.

Schafer, Robert, and Field, Charles G. "Section 235 of the National Housing
Act; Homeownership for Low Income Families?" JOURNAL OF URBAN LAW
46 (1969): 667-85.

Schafer and Field examine a government program to subsidize the
housing of low-income families. They criticize the program for
failing to consider the varying cost of construction and utilities
in different geographical sections of the country in establishing
the level of the subsidies.

Schechter, Alan H. "Impact of Open Housing Laws on Suburban Realtors."
URBAN AFFAIRS QUARTERLY 8 (June 1973): 439-64. Tables.

Schechter observes that the impact of federal and state laws upon
realtors in Boston suburbs has been minimal. Realtors continue to
restrict the information provided to blacks about housing opportunities in white neighborhoods and to discourage those who seek that
information.

Seeman, Isadore. "Give the Poor Credit: The Route in Homeownership."
JOURNAL OF HOUSING 25 (September 1968): 410-12.

Seeman observes that the most efficient method for achieving homeownership for the poor is the provision of federally subsidized mortgage credit.

Smolensky, Eugene. "Public Housing or Income Supplements--The Economics
of Housing for the Poor." JOURNAL OF THE AMERICAN INSTITUTE OF
PLANNERS 34 (March 1968): 94-101.

Smolensky finds that the goal of improving the quality of housing
for the poor can be achieved at a lower price by providing income
supplements to the poor rather than by the construction of new
dwellings. This tends to improve the poors' competitiveness in private housing markets.

Stegman, Michael A. "Slumlords and Public Policy." JOURNAL OF THE
AMERICAN INSTITUTE OF PLANNERS 33 (November 1967): 419-24.

Stegman observes that slum landlords do not make high profits.
Public housing projects disrupt the filtering process and worsen the
housing of low-income recipients in their effort to displace slum
landlords.

Sternlieb, George. "New York's Housing: A Study in Immobilism." PUBLIC
INTEREST, no. 16 (Summer 1969), pp. 123-38.

Since investment in new housing is deterred, Sternlieb finds that rent control in New York City benefits the white middle class and not ethnic minorities. By allowing market forces to operate, rents would increase and the stock of housing available for low-income families would increase as upper-income groups began to acquire higher-quality, higher-priced housing.

_____ . THE TENEMENT LANDLORD. New Brunswick, N.J.: Rutgers University Urban Studies Center, 1966. 269 p.

Sternlieb makes an extensive analysis of the operation of slum housing markets. He evaluates the effects of governmental controls and interventions in the housing market upon the quality of housing in slum areas. He concludes that market interventions have not improved and may have in fact worsened housing quality.

Sudman, Seymour, et al. "The Extent and Characteristics of Racially Integrated Housing in the United States." JOURNAL OF BUSINESS 42 (January 1969): 50-92. Tables.

The authors estimate that approximately 20 percent of the population of the United States lives in integrated neighborhoods. Property values do not decrease when integration occurs, and most integrated neighborhoods are composed of low-priced homes. Further, they estimate that the proportion of renters is higher in integrated neighborhoods than in segregated neighborhoods, since integrated neighborhoods tend to have a greater number of older homes. Most of the integrated neighborhoods, according to the authors, are located in the Northeast region of the country, and about one-third of the communities can be classified as suburban.

Taeuber, Karl [E.], and Taeuber, Alma F. NEGROES IN CITIES; RESIDENTIAL SEGREGATION AND NEIGHBORHOOD CHANGE. Chicago: Aldine Publishing Co., 1965. Tables. 284 p.

The Taeubers trace the evolution of housing segregation in Chicago. They demonstrate how blacks have been confined to certain sections of the city and have been unable to acquire housing outside of those districts. The policies of the City of Chicago Housing Authority and private realtors are largely responsible for the segregation.

"Techniques for Breaking Up America's Racial Ghettos." JOURNAL OF HOUSING 24 (October 1967): 505-10.

The article provides an excellent summary of various subsidy and incentive proposals for achieving integrated housing.

United States Commission on Civil Rights. CIVIL RIGHTS U.S.A. Washington, D.C.: 1962. 45 p. Sold by Government Printing Office.

The report investigates the extent of housing segregation in Washington, D.C., and examines the policies of the real estate industry which perpetuate the condition. The report also recommends government regulation of realtor practices.

Weissbourd, Bernard, and Channick, Herbert. "An Urban Strategy." CENTER MAGAZINE 1 (September 1968): 56–65.

Weissbourd and Channick develop a plan for achieving racially integrated residential areas through a system of subsidies and incentives for both blacks and whites. The political feasibility of such a scheme is, of course, extremely poor, especially in terms of paying whites to reside in integrated neighborhoods.

Williams, J. Allen, Jr. "The Effects of Urban Renewal on a Black Community." SOCIAL SCIENCE QUARTERLY 50 (December 1969): 703–12.

Williams finds that urban renewal has failed to attain its goals of improving housing quality, promoting racial integration, increasing urban property tax bases, and improving the social services received by the poor. Displaced families are usually forced to pay higher rents for their new residences. While one may view this as an improvement of housing quality, it is a choice that could have been made in the absence of urban renewal.

Willmann, John B. THE DEPARTMENT OF HOUSING AND URBAN DEVELOPMENT. New York: Frederick A. Praeger, Publishers, 1967. 207 p.

Willmann describes the structure and functions of the Department of Housing and Urban Development. Of interest are the portions dealing with programs to assist the poor.

Zelder, Raymond E. "Residential Desegregation--Can Nothing Be Accomplished?" URBAN AFFAIRS QUARTERLY 5 (March 1970): 265–77.

Zelder outlines a program to induce population relocation within urban areas so as to achieve racial integration. Among the proposals are the elimination of public housing projects, the elimination of government mortgage program subsidies, and the elimination of mortgage interest rate deductions from the federal income tax. Subsidies in the form of tax credits, direct cash payments, and reductions in mortgage payments should be given to those relocating so as to achieve integration.

Chapter 6

ECONOMIC DEVELOPMENT

OF THE BLACK COMMUNITY

Chapter 6
ECONOMIC DEVELOPMENT
OF THE BLACK COMMUNITY

Abrams, Elliott. "Black Capitalism and Black Banks." THE NEW LEADER 52 (March 17, 1969): 14-16.

Abrams observes that black-owned banks are small and few in number and rely heavily upon deposits from white businesses. Their service charges are often higher than white-owned banks, thereby discouraging black customers. As presently constituted, black banks cannot be viewed as a viable force in the development of black business enterprises.

Aldrich, Howard E. "Employment Opportunities for Blacks in the Black Ghetto: The Role of White-Owned Businesses." AMERICAN JOURNAL OF SOCIOLOGY 78 (May 1973): 1403-25.

Aldrich observes that whites own the majority of prosperous ghetto area businesses and are the major local employers. If their businesses expand, black employment opportunities should also improve. Therefore, the expansion of white-owned ghetto businesses is in the best interests of blacks.

Allen, Charles C. "The View from the Black Community." PLANNING AND ADVISORY SERVICE REPORT, no. 274 (November 1971), pp. 37-43.

Allen states that urban planning is conducted without significant participation of the black community. This nonparticipation has reached the point that many blacks view urban planning as conducted in a manner which is detrimental to the community's interests.

America, Richard F., Jr. "What Do You People Want?" HARVARD BUSINESS REVIEW (March/April 1969): 103-12.

America examines the income and wealth differentials between blacks and whites. As a remedial action, he proposes that the ownership of some major corporations be transferred to blacks. While this proposal would eliminate black poverty, so would other transfer schemes. The probability of this proposal being enacted is infinitesimal.

Aumente, Jerome. "Detroit Builds from the Ashes." THINK 35 (September/ October 1969): 15-17.

> Aumente describes the program of the New Detroit Committee, a
> group comprised of business, labor, religious, government, and
> civic leaders coordinated to remedy the conditions contributing to
> the 1967 riot in that city. The major effort has been the hiring
> of so-called hard-core unemployables via selection standards which
> did not penalize applicants with low educational attainment, crim-
> inal records, and poor work records. Training programs have also
> been instituted. Aumente also describes the efforts of the Eco-
> nomic Development Corporation of Detroit to supply management
> and financial expertise to black businessmen, provide venture
> capital, and obtain customers.

Bailey, Ron[ald W.]. "Economic Aspects of the Black Internal Colony." REVIEW OF BLACK POLITICAL ECONOMY 3 (Summer 1973): 43-72.

> According to Bailey, the surplus value resulting from the exploita-
> tion of black labor is being distributed to blacks in a minimal way
> --tokenism and welfare. That a distribution is even occurring is
> the result of the perceived threat to the white establishment.

_____, ed. BLACK BUSINESS ENTERPRISE--HISTORICAL AND CONTEMPO-RARY PERSPECTIVES. New York: Basic Books, 1971. 361 p. Tables.

> This is a book of readings containing articles on the historical
> development of black enterprises, whether black capitalism will
> or should work, and alternatives to black economic development.
> The book provides a valuable overview for the researcher.

Baron, Harold [M.]. "Black Powerlessness in Chicago." TRANSACTION 6 (November 1968): 27-33. Tables.

> While blacks comprised 20 percent of the population of Cook County,
> Illinois, they occupied only 2.6 percent of the policy-making posi-
> tions. The more powerful the position, the fewer the black policy
> makers. The best way to increase both the number and the power
> of black policy makers is through unifying the black constituency.

Baylor, John R. "The Ghetto's Need for Liability Insurance." KENTUCKY LAW JOURNAL 57 (1969): 676-86.

> Insurance companies are reluctant to insure ghetto dwellings, and
> when they do, higher premiums are charged than in nonghetto areas.
> Those who need insurance the most and can afford to pay the least
> pay the highest premiums. Government subsidization or require-
> ments that premiums be equalized between ghetto and nonghetto
> areas are possible solutions.

Beard, Samuel S. "Commitment Is a Red Herring." URBAN AFFAIRS QUARTERLY

6 (September 1970): 8-21.

> Beard observes that financial incentives are necessary in order to secure the involvement of private enterprise in black community development, and business should lobby for legislation which will allow it to enter the public sphere profitably.

Bell, Carolyn Shaw. THE ECONOMICS OF THE GHETTO. New York: Pegasus, 1970. 267 p.

> Bell examines income, employment, housing, and consumption data of ghetto areas and concludes that ghettos impose direct and indirect costs upon not only ghetto residents but all of society. Bell proposes breaking down the barriers to free trade between the ghetto and the rest of urban society.

Blackman, Courtney, N. "An Eclectic Approach to the Problem of Black Economic Development." THE REVIEW OF BLACK POLITICAL ECONOMY 2 (Fall 1971): 3-27.

> Blackman observes that the economy of black ghettos is stable at low levels of income. Economic growth is necessary, but the black economy is fragmented geographically and therefore defies a macro-economic solution. Such policies as broader capital financing, which allow black businesses to enter national markets, should be instituted.

Blaustein, Arthur S. "What is Community Economic Development?" URBAN AFFAIRS QUARTERLY 6 (September 1970): 52-70.

> Blaustein criticizes governmental efforts to promote minority business enterprises for building up false hope and not delivering. Black community groups will have to become more militant at the local level in order to make federal government minority business development programs more effective.

Bloom, Gordon F. "Black Capitalism in Ghetto Supermarkets: Problems and Prospects." INDUSTRIAL MANAGEMENT REVIEW 11 (Spring 1970): 37-48.

> According to Bloom, the cost of pilferage is higher in ghetto stores and contributes to noncompetitive pricing. The relatively low profit margins in the supermarket hardly contribute to the designation of the supermarket industry as a leading sector in black economic development.

Bluestone, Barry. "Black Capitalism: The Path to Black Liberation?" REVIEW OF RADICAL POLITICAL ECONOMICS 1 (May 1969): 36-55.

> Bluestone describes various methods for establishing black-owned and -operated businesses. All methods require the cooperation of white-dominated institutions. In assessing the success of black capitalism, the important criterion is the degree to which black political and social power increase. Because of the required co-

operation of white-dominated institutions, black capitalism will not yield black liberation.

Brazier, Arthur M. BLACK SELF-DETERMINATION: THE STORY OF THE WOODLAWN ORGANIZATION. Grand Rapids, Mich.: William B. Eerdmans Publishing Co., 1969. 148 p.

Brazier describes the development of an economic and political power base built by a black community organization in Chicago's Woodlawn neighborhood. The organization has had notable success in improving the employment of area youth and reducing street crime.

Brimmer, Andrew F. "Recent Developments in Black Banking: 1970-71." REVIEW OF BLACK POLITICAL ECONOMY 3 (Fall 1972): 58-73.

According to Brimmer's 1971 survey, black-owned banks acquired deposits at a faster rate than commercial banks. The average black bank, however, is about one-third the size of the average white-owned bank.

Brooks, Thomas R. "Workers, Black and White: Drumbeats in Detroit." DISSENT 17 (January/February 1970): 16-25.

Brooks describes a militant black workers group in the auto industry known as DRUM--the Dodge Revolutionary Union Movement. Since this article was written the organization has disbanded, largely as the result of members being fired after wildcat strikes which were not authorized by the United Automobile Workers Union. The article, however, provides an interesting perspective on black factionalism within unions and provides an insight into groups which have emulated DRUM within the auto industry.

Broom, Leonard, and Glenn, Norval D. TRANSFORMATION OF THE NEGRO AMERICAN. New York: Harper and Row, Publishers, 1965. xi, 207 p.

Broom and Glenn provide an historical description of the civil rights movement. The book is particularly valuable for its description of·changes in black strategy and government policy. The authors also discuss sociopsychological factors within the black community and changes over a period of time.

Browne, Robert S. "Barriers to Black Participation in the U.S. Economy." REVIEW OF BLACK POLITICAL ECONOMY 1 (Autumn 1970): 57-67.

Browne views redistribution of wealth through the payment of reparations to blacks as the most meaningful way of attaining black economic development. Browne concludes that black capitalism, within the present wealth distribution, will have little impact upon low-income blacks.

. "The Constellation of Politics and Economics: A Dynamic Duo in the Black Economy." REVIEW OF BLACK POLITICAL ECONOMY 2 (Fall 1971): 44-55.

Economic power has generally been the route to political power. Because blacks lack economic power but do have political power, it must be used to increase their share of the national income. If capital investment is not forthcoming domestically, the black community should appeal to foreign investors and world development organizations.

Christian, Charles M., and Bennett, Sari J. "Industrial Relocations from the Black Community of Chicago." GROWTH AND CHANGE 4 (April 1973): 14-20. Tables.

Christian and Bennett observe that firms relocating from black neighborhoods tend to select white neighborhoods. As a result of the fact that white neighborhoods were not accessible to blacks, they lost 7,000 jobs between 1969 and 1971 when relocation into white areas occured.

"Cleveland: The Hough Area Development Corporation." VISTA VOLUNTEER 5 (1969): 4-9.

This article describes black economic development efforts in Cleveland by a community organization founded after a civil disturbance in that city.

Coles, Flournoy A., Jr. "Financial Institutions and Black Entrepreneurship." JOURNAL OF BLACK STUDIES 3 (March 1973): 329-49.

The United States Small Business Administration has provided inadequate financing for black-owned businesses. Coles proposes the establishment of a Cabinet level department to foster black economic development through the provision of loans at subsidized rates of interest to businesses which would ordinarily be denied loans by conventional lending institutions.

Crandall, Robert W., and Mac Rae, C. Duncan. "Economic Subsidies in the Urban Ghetto." SOCIAL SCIENCE QUARTERLY 52 (December 1971): 492-507.

According to Crandall and Mac Rae, government subsidization of black economic development is inefficient, because capital is substituted for labor, while unemployment in ghettos is high and capital is diverted from more productive uses outside the ghetto. In order to reduce unemployment and raise incomes, wage subsidies should be utilized; they are more efficient and in the better interest of the black community than capital subsidies.

Cross, Theodore L. BLACK CAPITALISM. New York: Atheneum, 1969. 274 p.

Among the obstacles to the growth of black-owned businesses

are lack of venture capital and entrepreneurial skills. A vast restructuring of capital markets and training of black managers are necessary prerequisites. Cross suggests programs for whites to assist black entrepreneurs in production, marketing, and financing.

Danzig, David. "The Racial Explosion in American Society." NEW UNIVERSITY THOUGHT 5 (January 1967): 30-45.

Danzig advocates the establishment of black-controlled civil rights organizations in all sectors of society where the position of blacks is unequal.

Davis, Earl F., et al. "Establishment of a Minority Small Business Training Program: In Retrospect." MSU TOPICS 21 (Spring 1973): 64-72.

The authors describe an unsuccessful program to develop black entrepreneurs. A possible research topic is whether the program failed as a result of improper methods of instruction, or whether it is an invalid assumption that entrepreneurship can be developed.

Davis, Homer. THE STAKE OF MINORITIES IN COMMUNITY ACTION. Morgantown: Institute for Labor Studies, West Virginia University, 1967. 22 p.

Blacks comprise a larger proportion of the target groups for community action programs than their proportion within the country's population. Their participation in the planning, implementation, and evaluation stages of the programs is vital to the success of community action.

Doctors, Samuel S., and Juris, Harvey A. "Management and Technical Assistance for Minority Enterprise." URBAN AFFAIRS QUARTERLY 7 (June 1972): 473-87.

Doctors and Juris observe that the government training policy should distinguish between training minority entrepreneurs and training minority managers, because the needs of the two groups are different. Entrepreneurs require broader knowledge of methods of securing financial capital and overall business operations than do managers.

Donaldson, Loraine, and Strangways, Raymond S. "Can Ghetto Groceries Price Competitively and Make a Profit?" THE JOURNAL OF BUSINESS 46 (January 1973): 61-65.

According to Donaldson and Strangways, a standard market basket cannot be used to determine whether or not the poor pay more than higher income groups for food, because the poor purchase different food items. However, the poor pay more in terms of markups over cost on their market basket items. This product mix effect enables the ghetto grocer to price competitively with firms outside the ghetto.

Douglas, Pamela. "Black Television: Avenues of Power." BLACK SCHOLAR 5 (September 1973): 23-31.

> Douglas observes that blacks are absent from the managerial ranks of the television industry, and black ownership of stations is hampered by financial and political obstacles.

Downs, Anthony. "Alternative Futures for the American Ghetto." DAEDALUS 97 (Fall 1968): 1331-78.

> Upon examining alternative strategies for improving the ghetto, Downs finds them to be inadequate and advocates the dispersal of blacks into white residential areas.

Emeka, Mauris L. "Black Banks: Progress and Problems." NEW YORK TIMES, June 10, 1973, Section 3, p. 1.

> According to Emeka, the profitability of black-owned banks is improving. Emeka indicates that a major problem is the failure to make loans to black-owned businesses for expansion and concentration on consumer loans for durable goods such as automobiles and home appliances.

Farley, Rawle. "Black Banking: A Comment on the Andrew Brimmer Bias." REVIEW OF BLACK POLITICAL ECONOMY 2 (Spring 1972): 45-55.

> Fostering black banks in the mold of banks serving the white community will not maximize black economic development. According to Farley, banks emulating those in developing countries would be more effective. His criticisms are aimed at proposals of a black member on the Federal Reserve Board of Governors.

Ferry W.H. "Farewell to Integration." CENTER MAGAZINE 1 (March 1968): 35-40.

> Ferry interprets the mood of blacks as one of disdain for racial integration and preference for the construction of separate black-controlled economic, social, and political institutions.

Franklin, Raymond S. "The Political Economy of Black Power." SOCIAL PROBLEMS 16 (Winter 1969): 286-301.

> Black power awakens blacks and whites to the contradictions of capitalistic society. Governmental programs, as presently constituted, are a patchwork policy resulting in tokenism and welfare. An effective response to black power, according to Franklin, necessitates a basic restructuring of capitalism.

Friesema, H. Paul. "Black Control of Central Cities: The Hollow Prize." JOURNAL OF THE AMERICAN INSTITUTE OF PLANNERS 35 (March 1969): 75-79.

> Friesema observes that blacks are the last of the racial and ethnic

minority groups to migrate to the cities. In many central cities, they comprise a majority of the electorate and have elected, or in the near future will elect, public officials. Unfortunately, the emergence of this political power base is occurring at a time when the economic condition of central cities is deteriorating due to the declining fortunes of firms located in the cities and the movement of commercial activity to the suburbs.

Fusfeld, Daniel R. "Anatomy of the Ghetto Economy." NEW GENERATION 51 (Summer 1969): 2-6.

Fusfeld observes that the sources of income to the residents of black ghettos are illegal activities, declining sectors of the economy, and government transfer payments. Revenue is drained from the ghetto economy by banks and other businesses which invest in nonghetto areas. He advocates community control of the ghetto economy.

_____. THE BASIC ECONOMICS OF THE URBAN RACIAL CRISIS. New York: Holt, Rinehart and Winston, 1973. 122 p. Tables and charts.

Fusfeld describes the relationship of the ghetto to the surrounding metropolitan area, the effects of black migration and the population explosion within the ghetto, the operation of the ghetto economy, the role of the welfare system in the ghetto, and black and white capitalism in the ghetto. He utilizes a coerced labor theory to examine the situation of blacks in urban labor markets. Full employment, increases in the minimum wage, training and retraining, a guaranteed annual income, and ghetto economic development are all necessary programs for the elimination of the black-white income inequality.

Garnett, Bernard. "Black Bankers Foresee Growth." RACE RELATIONS RE-PORTER 2 (November 1, 1971): 11-21.

Garnett chronicles the improved condition of black-owned banks in recent years. Deposits have grown at a faster rate than for white-owned banks. While black banks are comparatively small, continued growth is anticipated.

_____. "Black Banking in the Black Community." RACE RELATIONS RE-PORTER 3 (January 3, 1972): 1-8.

Black-owned banks incur substantially higher costs of handling a given level of deposits than white banks. A major reason for the relatively low deposits of black banks is the failure of large portions of the black community to utilize their services.

_____. "Black Insurance: From a Barber Shop to a Billion Dollars." RACE RELATIONS REPORTER 3 (May 1972): 1-7.

Black-owned companies, according to Garnett, are the most prosperous black enterprises. Their role in fostering further black economic development has been minimal because of the high proportion of loans to consumers.

Gibson, James. "Ghetto Economic Development: New Ways of Giving Non-Whites the Business?" CIVIL RIGHTS DIGEST 2 (Spring 1969): 9-14.

Gibson examines the issue of whether "black economic development" is merely a placebo offered by whites to quell black unrest. Opportunities exist, but the potential impact upon black income inequality may not be great.

Ginzberg, Eli, ed. BUSINESS LEADERSHIP AND THE NEGRO CRISIS. New York: McGraw-Hill Book Co., 1968. 175 p.

The book consists of a group of articles on ways that the white business community can improve the economic condition of blacks. A major premise of the book is that stability of the urban environment is of concern to business, and it must be willing to pay for that condition in order to achieve long-run profitability. This "anti-riot" strategy of the late 1960s has lost its fervor as summers have become cooler.

Glasgow, Douglas. "Black Power through Community Control." SOCIAL WORK 17 (May 1972): 56-64.

The black community has suffered from the absence of self-determination. In attempting to gain community control of institutions, blacks are not departing from the concept of power blocs utilized by other interest groups.

Glazer, Nathan. "Blacks and Ethnic Groups: The Difference, and the Political Difference it Makes." SOCIAL PROBLEMS 18 (Spring 1971): 444-61.

Except for the Irish, there appears to be a strong analogy between the experience of blacks and white ethnic groups in attaining economic and political power. Neither blacks nor white ethnics have been successful at securing political power.

Green, Gerson, and Faux, Geoffrey. "The Social Utility of Black Enterprise." In BLACK ECONOMIC DEVELOPMENT, pp. 21-37. Edited by William F. Haddad and G. Douglas Pugh. Englewood Cliffs, N.J.: Prentice-Hall, 1969.

Although there is agreement that the development of black enterprise is necessary, there is little actual program experience upon which to judge the scale and type of programs. Development strategies can be categorized as either separatist or integrationist. Green and Faux recognize the need for establishing the means for evaluating development strategies which will account for social costs and benefits attributable to both strategies.

Haber, Alan. "Economic Development: Liberation or Liberalism." NEW

GENERATION 50 (Spring 1968): 18-21.

Haber observes that corporate and government proposals for ghetto economic development do not contemplate either displacing the white-owned core of the ghetto economy, surrendering investment decisions to the ghetto, subsidizing political organization, sacrificing market return on investment, or excluding themselves from markets they generate. The best interests of blacks will not be served as long as development proposals disregard these aspects.

Haddad, William F., and Pugh, G. Douglas, eds. BLACK ECONOMIC DE-VELOPMENT. Englewood Cliffs, N.J.: Prentice-Hall, 1969. 176 p. Tables.

Of particular value in this book of readings are articles on the evaluation of black economic development programs, rates of return to black enterprises, local development corporations, and bonding of minority contractors.

Harris, Philip. "Franchising for Minorities: An Avenue into the Economic Mainstream." CIVIL RIGHTS DIGEST 3 (Winter 1970): 32-37.

Since minorities own a relatively small proportion of franchised businesses, Harris recommends active recruitment and training of minorities. This proposal will probably not receive serious consideration today because of publicized deficiencies in the franchising system.

Harrison, Bennett. "Economic Development Planning for American Urban Slums." INTERNATIONAL DEVELOPMENT REVIEW 10 (March 1968): 23-29.

Harrison's analysis treats Harlem as if it is an underdeveloped country; an unfavorable balance of payments and a low economic growth rate are common characteristics of both. Harrison describes a development bank plan for Harlem, and cites as a major goal import substitution. The instruments for change are investment in new and expanded businesses and job training.

Hatcher, Richard G. "Mass Media and the Black Community." BLACK SCHOLAR 5 (September 1973): 2-10.

Blacks are underrepresented in employment and ownership within the media industry. A consequence is misinformation and disregard of the black community by the media. The heavy capital investment required appears to be a major obstacle to increased black ownership.

Hatchett, John F. "The Negro Revolution: A Quest for Justice?" JOURNAL OF HUMAN RELATIONS 14 (Third Quarter, 1966): 406-21.

Heilbrun, James, and Conant, Roger R. "Profitability and Size of Firm as Evidence of Dualism in the Black Ghetto." URBAN AFFAIRS QUARTERLY 7 (March 1972): 251-84.

In Harlem, black-owned businesses are less profitable than white-owned businesses. If the supply of capital to black entrepreneurs is increased, expansion into the profitable white sector can be expected. A problem with this conclusion is the possibility that white consumers will discriminate against black-owned businesses in making purchases. An alternative is consolidation of existing black businesses in order to achieve economies of scale.

Heilbrun, James, and Wellisz, Stanislaw. "An Economic Program for the Ghetto." In URBAN RIOTS: VIOLENCE AND SOCIAL CHANGE, pp. 72-85. Edited by Robert H. Connery. New York: Columbia University, 1968.

Heilbrun and Wellisz examine various strategies for promoting the economic development of the ghetto, which is treated as an economic entity. They discuss development in a framework similar to that for underdeveloped countries. Increased investment in both capital and human resources is the key feature of this plan.

Henderson, William L., and Ledebur, Larry C. "Programs for the Economic Development of the American Negro Community: The Moderate Approach." AMERICAN JOURNAL OF ECONOMICS AND SOCIOLOGY 30 (January 1971): 27-45.

Henderson and Ledebur review proposals designed to promote black economic development within the context of the American institutional structure. These proposals require the cooperative participation of government and business. Their success, therefore, is contingent upon the participation of institutions which also share the burden for the economic inequality of blacks.

_____. "The Viable Alternative for Black Economic Development." PUBLIC POLICY 18 (Spring 1970): 429-49.

Henderson and Ledebur examine job training and placement, black capitalism, and dispersal from the ghetto as three alternatives for black economic advancement. The first is limited by insufficient demand for black labor within the ghetto. The second maintains the ghetto whose market is deficient for economic development. The authors prefer the integrationist strategy, because dispersal of blacks from the ghetto will enable them to enter the developed market of white society.

Holden, Matthew. "Black Politicians in the Time of the New Urban Politics." REVIEW OF BLACK POLITICAL ECONOMY 2 (Fall 1971): 56-71.

Holden identifies elected offices which are sources of power but often neglected by blacks. Since many urban problems can only be solved through national policy, cities must receive special status by the federal government, thereby increasing their representation in Congress.

Hunter, Charlayne. "The New Black Businessman." SATURDAY REVIEW (August

23, 1969): 27-29.

Hunter describes some successful black enterprises. The article suggests factors for analysis when forecasting the probability of success of proposed black enterprises.

Jones, Edward H. BLACKS IN BUSINESS. New York: Grosset and Dunlap, 1971. 214 p. Tables.

Jones traces the development of the black business community. He examines problems of capital formation, credit, insurance, and managerial efficiency, and prescribes the support of government and white-owned businesses in order to surmount these deficiencies.

Kafoglis, Madelyn L. "The Economics of Community Action." THE TENNESSEE SURVEY OF BUSINESS 3 (December 1967): 1-7.

The Community Action Program has failed to achieve its goal of enlisting the voluntary participation of residents of affected areas. Kafoglis attributes the cost of this failure to the voluntary nature of the program, which does not adequately compensate for participation costs.

Kain, J[ohn] F., and Persky, J[oseph] J. "Alternatives to the Gilded Ghetto." THE PUBLIC INTEREST 14 (Winter 1969): 74-87.

Discrimination concentrates blacks into urban ghettos. Among the alternatives for eliminating the ghetto are suburbanization through housing legislation, busing ghetto children to suburban schools, and the establishment of job opportunities outside the central city. These alternatives are better than policies designed to build the economic base of the ghetto.

Klein, Richard. "A Synergism: Business Students and the Disadvantaged Entrepreneur." ATLANTA ECONOMIC REVIEW 21 (October 1971): 32-35.

Klein describes a consulting service for minority businessmen provided by graduate students in business administration. This program, which provides students the opportunity to apply knowledge acquired in the classroom, appears to benefit both the students and the minority businessmen.

Labrie, Peter. "Black Central Cities: Dispersal or Rebuilding--Part I." REVIEW OF BLACK POLITICAL ECONOMY 1 (Autumn 1970): 3-27.

Labrie disagrees with the proposal that the dispersal of blacks throughout urban areas is the most effective means for improving their economic condition. He emphasizes the reconstruction of ghetto areas, because any economic viability which blacks do enjoy is a result of concerted action and geographic concentration.

Larson, Calvin J., and Hill, Richard J. "Segregation, Community Consciousness, and Black Power." JOURNAL OF BLACK STUDIES 2 (March 1972): 263-76.

> Larson and Hill observe that the more segregated the black com-
> munity, the greater the community consciousness and cohesiveness
> among its residents. The implication of this conclusion is that the
> opportunity for community development efforts is greater in more
> segregated localities.

Levitan, Sar A., and Taggert, Robert III. "Developing Business in the Ghetto."
CONFERENCE BOARD RECORD 6 (July 1969): 13-21.

> Levitan and Taggert identify obstacles to the development of business
> enterprise in the ghetto. These include high labor turnover, pil-
> ferage, and restrictive zoning ordinances.

_____. "Ghetto Business Development--Performance and Prospects." MAN-
POWER 1 (September 1969): 2-8.

> Levitan and Taggert state that among the major problems confront-
> ing ghetto business development are the high cost of land in the
> central cities, the high cost of training disadvantaged workers,
> and the disinclination of white business executives to work in the
> ghetto. They view large manufacturing firms as the most likely to
> locate in the ghetto.

Levy, Burton. "The Bureaucracy of Race: Enforcement of Civil Rights Laws
and Its Impact on People, Process, and Organization." JOURNAL OF BLACK
STUDIES 2 (September 1971): 77-105. Tables.

> Levy observes that black bureaucrats are more militant than the
> general black population as a result of seeing how wasted their
> efforts are. Militancy within the black community would increase
> if communication about the failure of government programs were
> more direct.

Light, Ivan H. ETHNIC ENTERPRISE IN AMERICA: BUSINESS AND WELFARE
AMONG CHINESE, JAPANESE, AND BLACKS. Berkeley, Calif.: University
of California Press, 1972. 209 p. Tables.

> Light traces the development of black, Chinese, and Japanese
> business enterprises with particular emphasis upon financial insti-
> tutions within the communities. He examines the roles of commun-
> ity organizations such as the kenjin in Japanese society, the im-
> migrant brotherhoods in Chinese society, and the Urban League and
> Business League in black society. The value of this study is that
> it provides an understanding of how a minority can provide self-
> sustaining financial support for community business enterprises.

McClelland, David C. "Black Capitalism: Making it Work." THINK 35
(July/August, 1969): 6-11.

> McClelland describes the motivational problems prevalent within
> the black culture after generations of discriminatory treatment.

Improving the achievement motivation of potential black entrepreneurs is a necessary prerequisite for the success of black capitalism.

McClory, Robert. "Rough Times in Minority Business." RACE RELATIONS RE-PORTER 4 (April 23, 1973): 5-8.

McClory attributes the high failure rate of black-owned businesses to poor management, inadequate finances, and lack of support from the black community. The value of this article is that it presents hypotheses which researchers may test empirically.

McKersie, Robert B. "The Civil Rights Movement and Employment." INDUS-TRIAL RELATIONS 3 (May 1964): 1-21.

According to McKersie, the civil rights movement is analogous to the CIO organizing drives of the 1930s in terms of tactics. With particular attention to the direct action approach, McKersie ex-amines the tactics of civil rights groups with varying degrees of militancy, from that of the National Urban League to that of the Congress of Racial Equality. Just as organizing tactics are similar to those of the labor movement, so are many of the negotiating tactics employed by civil rights leaders.

_____. "Vitalize Black Enterprise." HARVARD BUSINESS REVIEW 46 (Sep-tember/October, 1968): 88-99.

McKersie describes governmental, white-dominated business, and black civil rights group efforts to foster the development of black businesses. Development requires the opening of new business op-portunities, the infusion of sufficient capital, and the application of managerial know-how.

McLemore, Leslie Burl. "Toward a Theory of Black Politics--The Black and Ethnic Models Revisited." JOURNAL OF BLACK STUDIES 2 (March 1972): 323-31.

McLemore denies that blacks can utilize the path of political power followed by white ethnic groups. Racism and the inability of blacks to be assimilated due to skin color are the major reasons.

Madway, David. "Minority Enterprise Financing--Mired or Moving?" REVIEW OF BLACK POLITICAL ECONOMY 3 (Fall 1972): 87-93.

According to Madway, inability to adequately service debt is the major reason black-owned businesses fail. Madway's suggested re-medial action is an increased subsidization by the government which would reduce the failure rate of minority enterprises.

Marshall, Kenneth E. "Goals of the Black Community." In GOVERNING THE CITY: CHANGES AND OPTIONS FOR NEW YORK, pp. 193-205. Edited by Robert H. Connery and Demetrios Caraley. New York: Academy of Politi-cal Science, 1969.

Marshall forecasts that the struggle for black equality will occur increasingly in the large cities. He proposes an overhaul of anti-poverty agencies and community action groups so that they are more responsive to the needs of the minority community.

Mitchell, Daniel B. "Black Economic Development and Income Drain: The Case of Numbers." REVIEW OF BLACK POLITICAL ECONOMY 1 (Autumn 1970): 47-56.

Mitchell proposes black control and legalization of the "numbers game" as a source of capital for black economic development. The numbers game is one of the most viable business enterprises in the black community. Under present conditions, profits are not invested in business enterprises within the community but are diverted to consumption and sources outside the community.

Morsell, John A. "The National Association for the Advancement of Colored People and Its Strategy." ANNALS OF THE AMERICAN ACADEMY OF POLITICAL AND SOCIAL SCIENCES 357 (January 1965): 97-101.

The National Association for the Advancement of Colored People has been at the forefront of the civil rights movement during this century. During most of its existence, its primary strategy was the conduction of court cases. In recent years, it has been inclined to take more direct action.

New Detroit Committee. PROGRESS REPORT OF THE NEW DETROIT COMMITTEE. Detroit, Mich.: Metropolitan Fund, 1968. 23 p.

The report details efforts to improve the socioeconomic status of blacks in Detroit by an organization comprised of business, civic, and labor leaders. It is interesting to note the enthusiastic outlook presented in this report in view of the fact that the organization is an admitted failure today.

O'Neal, Frederick. "The Role of the Black Trade Unionist." AMERICAN FEDERATIONIST 77 (July 1970): 9-12.

O'Neal specifies his view of the ideal black trade unionist as being a militant, nonviolent integrationist who is politically active. Black capitalism, community control, and tax incentives to white corporations for ghetto economic development are dismissed as against the best interests of blacks.

Parris, Guichard, and Brook, Lester. BLACKS IN THE CITY: A HISTORY OF THE NATIONAL URBAN LEAGUE. Boston: Little, Brown & Co., 1971. 534 p.

The National Urban League continues to be the most moderate of civil rights organizations. Its primary goal is the improvement of black socioeconomic conditions through cooperation with white employers. While subject to increasing criticism in recent years by militants, the League has served a useful purpose.

Pascal, Anthony H. "Black Gold and Black Capitalism." PUBLIC INTEREST, no. 19 (Spring 1970), pp. 111-19.

Blacks have been unable to emulate other ethnic groups by dominating particular industries. Such industries must possess the potential for individual enterprise and be easy to enter. The gasoline service station business fulfills the criteria. Pascal fails, however, to note the high failure rate in the industry and paucity of investment capital in the black community.

Phemister, James M., and Hildebrand, James L. "The Use of Non-Profit Corporations and Cooperatives for Ghetto Economic Development." JOURNAL OF URBAN LAW 48 (1970-71): 181-231.

Phemister and Hildebrand compare nonprofit corporations with cooperatives as vehicles for achieving both community control and economic development. Nonprofit corporations are more advantageous than cooperatives because of the greater latitude afforded by the law.

Rendon, Armando. "Portland Blacks Get Their Company Thing Together." CIVIL RIGHTS DIGEST 2 (Spring 1969): 15-25.

Rendon describes the experiences of a black-owned and -operated company in Portland, Oregon, and the obstacles it has overcome in order to achieve economic viability.

Rodman, Hyman. "The Lower Classes and the Negroes: Implications for Intellectuals." In NEW PERSPECTIVES ON POVERTY, pp. 168-172. Edited by Arthur B. Shostak and William Gomberg. Englewood Cliffs, N.J.: Prentice-Hall, 1965.

Unlike blacks, lower-socioeconomic-class whites lack effective spokesmen. Bitterness and conflict between the groups is certain unless intellectuals act as the spokesmen for both groups.

Rosen, Alex. "The Deepening Crisis in Intergroup Relations." THE JOURNAL OF INTERGROUP RELATIONS 4 (Summer 1965): 105-18.

Rosen chronicles many of the conflicts which exist between blacks and whites. Recognition of common problems and cooperative efforts between races are advocated.

Rosen, Sumner M. "Better Mousetraps--Reflections on Economic Development in the Ghetto." URBAN REVIEW 4 (May 1970): 14-18.

Rosen criticizes the black separatist view of economic development as unrealistic. Financial and political power is greater through white alliances.

Rustin, Bayard. "From Protest to Politics: The Future of the Civil Rights Movement." COMMENTARY 39 (February 1965): 25-31.

> Rustin stresses a coalition between blacks and white liberals to increase the involvement of the public sector in economic and educational reform. Public works projects are viewed as a possible tool.

Sabin, Dennis P. "Why Increase Citizen Participation among Ghetto Residents?" JOURNAL OF BLACK STUDIES 2 (March 1972): 359-70.

> Input of ghetto residents in the formulation and administration of programs for improving their socioeconomic condition is necessary because they are in a position to evaluate the effectiveness of the programs. A problem with this conclusion is the assumption that government-sponsored programs are intended to improve what the black community perceives to be its needs.

Samuels, Howard. "How to Even the Odds." SATURDAY REVIEW, August 23, 1969, pp. 22-26.

> Samuels examines black capitalism and recommends the infusion of investment by government and the private sector. Government training programs and the lending of technical expertise by white businesses are also necessary.

Santiestevan, Henry. "Fresh Wind in the Ghetto." IUD AGENDA 3 (February 1967): 9-12.

> Santiestevan dexcribes the operation of a tenant's union in Chicago and the collective bargaining process with landlords. He concludes that the process is an effective means for improving the housing of minorities.

Schaffer, Richard Lance. INCOME FLOWS IN URBAN POVERTY AREAS. Lexington, Mass.: Lexington Books, 1973. 128 p. Tables.

> Schaffer analyzes the flow of income to and expenditures from ghetto areas. Income is not retained within the ghetto communities, and their continual economic decline is certain unless the flow of money out of the ghettos is tempered. Alternative strategies for reducing the outflow are possible topics of investigation for the researcher.

Singer, Neil M. "Federal Aid to Minority Business: Survey and Critique." SOCIAL SCIENCE QUARTERLY 54 (September 1973): 292-305.

> According to Singer, federal government expansion of financial assistance to minority-owned business is necessary. Technical assistance, however, is best provided by white-owned businesses which have a greater understanding of the complexities of business enterprise and are more adept at solving operational problems.

Smolin, Ronald P. "A Ghetto's Quest for Economic Growth." COMMUNITIES IN ACTION 5 (February 1969): 4-7.

Spear, Allan H. BLACK CHICAGO--THE MAKING OF A NEGRO GHETTO. Chicago: University of Chicago Press, 1967. 254 p.

Spear describes the social, political, and economic policies and institutions which resulted in the concentration of blacks in low-income, segregated neighborhoods within Chicago. Of particular interest are the examples of de jure discrimination. The belief that the ghetto is solely the result of de facto discrimination is fallacious. By understanding the causes of ghettoization, the researcher should be prepared to formulate policies for the vitalization or dissolution of the ghetto.

Spitz, A. E. "Ghetto Retailing--Entrepreneurial Dilemma." ATLANTA ECONOMIC REVIEW 21 (October 1971): 36-37.

According to Spitz, black retailers face severe problems with bank credit, customer credit defaults, shoplifting, and robbery. Government subsidies are necessary to foster development.

Stewart, Douglas E. "Population, Environment, and Minority Groups." In POPULATION, ENVIRONMENT, AND PEOPLE, pp. 104-12. Edited by Noel Hinrichs. New York: McGraw-Hill Book Co., 1971.

Population control is in the best interests of black people and will not lead to further subjugation. Stewart suggests that by limiting family size, blacks should be able to better afford advanced training beyond high school and, thereby, be able to acquire economic power.

Stone, Chuck. BLACK POLITICAL POWER IN AMERICA. Indianapolis: Bobbs-Merrill Co., 1968. 215 p.

The major source of black political power has been outside the mainstream--boycotts versus elections. Hence, blacks are under-represented in public officialdom. Stone advises blacks to participate in elections and demand more patronage.

_____. "The White Foundation's Role in Black Oppression." BLACK SCHOLAR 3 (November 1971): 29-31.

Tax exempt foundations sponsor research and programs which are irrelevant to the needs of the black community. In order to maintain tax exempt status, political action must be avoided. Because of this legal constraint, the most effective path to black economic development is not followed.

Sturdivant, Frederick D. "The Limits of Black Capitalism. HARVARD BUSINESS REVIEW 47 (January/February 1969): 122-28.

In order to develop black capitalism, tax incentives, investment guarantees, and a greater availability of capital are necessary. Along with vigorous government action in terms of capitalization, development of managerial and entrepreneurial skills is a prerequisite. "Black capitalism" should mean the elimination of barriers to black enterprise, but not the reinforcement of presently inefficient ghetto enterprises.

Tabb, William K. "Government Incentives to Locate in Urban Poverty Areas." LAND ECONOMICS 45 (November 1969): 392-99.

Tabb states that the three arguments for federal subsidies to firms for locating in ghetto areas are the infant industry, spread effect, and wasted worker effect. Subsidies are inefficient from an equity and spatial distribution standpoint. He advocates black control of subsidized enterprises in order to retain a greater share of the benefits within the community, as opposed to control by white nonghetto residents.

_____. THE POLITICAL ECONOMY OF THE BLACK GHETTO. New York: W.W. Norton & Co., 1970. 152 p.

Tabb examines housing in the ghetto and government housing policy, which perpetuates the ghetto. The ghetto is treated as an internal colony within urban areas. Policies generally thought appropriate only for underdeveloped countries are applicable for the ghetto. Tabb discusses policies for developing black business enterprise, locating white dominated firms in the ghetto, supplementing the income of poor blacks, and developing the ghetto labor force.

_____. "Race Relations Models and Social Change." SOCIAL PROBLEMS 18 (Spring 1971): 431-43.

Whether an integrationist or separatist strategy is followed, the most important ingredient for improving the economic condition of blacks is the development of a viable black-owned business sector.

_____. "Viewing Minority Economic Development as a Problem in Political Economy." AMERICAN ECONOMIC REVIEW 62 (May 1972): 31-37.

As during World War II, tight labor market periods offer blacks the opportunity for economic gains. Because tight labor market periods are not sustained, a community development approach whereby resources of the community are harnessed to achieve economic growth is necessary in the long run.

Tate, Charles, ed. CABLE TELEVISION IN THE CITIES: COMMUNITY CONTROL, PUBLIC ACCESS, AND MINORITY OWNERSHIP. Washington, D.C.: Urban Institute, 1972. 184 p.

If present trends continue, blacks will not own cable television systems, nor have significant input into those already serving their communities. The implication of this conclusion is that black control over black communities will be difficult without significant input into this important communication source.

Tillman, James A., Jr., and Tillman, Mary Norman. "Black Intellectuals, White Liberals, and Race Relations: An Analytic Overview." PHYLON 33 (Spring 1972): 54-66.

The Tillmans observe that black intellectuals and white liberals have failed to improve race relations by leading fad-type movements, which they viewed as panaceas. These are education, employment, housing, compensatory education, and the study of black history. The real issue of white racism has received little attention.

Timmons, Jeffry A. "Black Is Beautiful—Is It Bountiful?" HARVARD BUSINESS REVIEW 49 (November/December 1971): 81-94.

According to Timmons, blacks participating in achievement motivation courses displayed significant improvements in entrepreneurial performance. Timmons, however, fails to indicate whether the courses themselves improved the entrepreneurial performance of the participants, or whether participation in the course indicates a higher achievement motivation than that of nonparticipants.

Travis, Dempsey J. "Barriers to Black Power in the American Economy." BLACK SCHOLAR 3 (November 1971): 21-25.

Travis enumerates the relatively small proportion of blacks comprising the capitalist class. The impoverished condition of the black community retards motivation and the availability of capital. A circular condition of poverty and discrimination immobilizes efforts to improve the black economic condition.

_____. "The Black Businessman: Obstacles to His Success." BLACK SCHOLAR 4 (January 1973): 19-21.

Travis states that black businessmen are supported by black consumers. They have attained limited penetration of white markets outside the ghetto. Penetration of white markets is necessary for economic growth, because income levels within the ghetto are inadequate to maintain a high degree of economic development.

United States Department of Labor, Manpower Administration. NEGRO EMPLOYMENT IN THE SOUTH. Vol. 2: THE MEMPHIS LABOR MARKET. Washington, D.C.: U.S. Government Printing Office, 1971. 57 p. Tables.

Blacks comprise a relatively small proportion of higher-paying occupations in the Memphis labor market. This condition is attributable to employer discrimination, housing segregation, and low educational attainment. Emerging black community organizations may alter this situation, according to the report.

Vietorisz, Thomas, and Harrison, Bennett. THE ECONOMIC DEVELOPMENT
OF HARLEM. New York: Frederick A. Praeger, Publishers, 1970. 287 p.

> Vietorisz and Harrison contend that the potential for an economi-
> cally developed ghetto exists. Development must be coordinated
> not from the objective of maximum profit but that of greatest eco-
> nomic development. Political power through unified community
> action will allow maximum development to occur.

_____. "Ghetto Development, Community Corporations, and Public Policy."
REVIEW OF BLACK POLITICAL ECONOMY 2 (Fall 1971): 28-43.

> According to Vietorisz and Harrison, profitability, the traditional
> stimulus of investment and subsequent development, may not be
> sufficient to promote ghetto economic development. Community
> development corporations, which organize and channel investment
> funds on the basis of community service, are necessary. Only
> after the traditional approach fails will the latter occur.

Wallich, Henry C., and Dodson, William J. "Economic Models and Black
Economic Development." REVIEW OF BLACK POLITICAL ECONOMY 3 (Fall
1972): 74-86.

> The white-nonwhite income differential is examined by Wallich and
> Dodson under various theoretical constructs. Equalizing educational
> and job market information channels between blacks and whites by
> government action will not result in equalized incomes as long as
> there is discrimination. Control of sufficient capital to employ all
> black labor in an occupational distribution similar to that for whites
> would equalize incomes.

Warren, Roland L., ed. POLITICS AND THE GHETTOS. New York: Atherton
Press, 1969. 214 p.

> Warren asserts the political system creates and perpetuates ghettos.
> As black communities continue to grow and to constitute a larger
> proportion of the electorate, the influence of blacks on the political
> process and conditions under which they live can be more directly
> under their control.

Widick, B. J. "Black City, Black Unions?" DISSENT 19 (Winter 1972): 138-
45.

> According to Widick, blacks will comprise a majority of Detroit's
> population. Their median income is the highest in the country.
> They comprise a significant portion of the unionized labor force
> and may emerge as a politically powerful group. This emergence,
> however, occurs at a time when the economic base of Detroit is
> declining.

_____. "Minority Power Through Unions." NATION 209 (September 8, 1969):
206-8.

Blacks are comprising an ever increasing proportion of many unions, particularly those in mass production industries. While still under-represented in leadership ranks, the possibility of the labor movement providing an impetus to black economic power exists.

Wiley, Peter, and Leman, Beverly. "Crisis in the Cities: Part One, the Business of Urban Reform." LEVIATHAN 1 (March 1969): 11-13.

Wiley and Leman speculate that the future of "black capitalism" may not be in black ownership of ghetto enterprises but in black administration of white owned firms operating in the ghetto. Given the difficulties confronting blacks in obtaining investment capital, this prospect appears to be quite feasible.

Winegarden, C. R. "Industrialization of the 'Black Economy': Industry Selection." REVIEW OF BLACK POLITICAL ECONOMY 1 (Autumn 1970): 28-46.

Winegarden selects manufacturing industries most capable of promoting black economic development. He uses three criteria in making his selections: labor intensity, the profitability of small production units, and the industry's rate of growth.

Yaspan, Robert. "Property Insurance and the American Ghetto: A Study in Social Irresponsibility." SOUTHERN CALIFORNIA LAW REVIEW 44 (Fall 1970): 218-74.

Yaspan observes that the property insurance fee structure impedes the economic development of ghetto areas by placing a proportionately heavier burden upon black-owned enterprises which are already weaker financially than nonghetto businesses. Equalization of fees between ghetto and nonghetto enterprises would equally distribute the social cost of maintaining ghetto crime and poverty.

Zweig, Michael. "The Dialectics of Black Capitalism." REVIEW OF BLACK POLITICAL ECONOMY 2 (Spring 1972): 25-37.

According to Zweig, a policy of fostering black capitalism will create a class structure within black society similar to that in white society. Community participation is not likely to prevent this result. Subsidies to black-owned businesses are inefficient. The incidence of the taxes needed to pay subsidies would be greatest upon the white working class. The result would be an intensification of interracial strife.

Chapter 7

BLACK CONSUMERS

Chapter 7

BLACK CONSUMERS

Alexis, Marcus. "Patterns of Black Consumption 1935-1960." JOURNAL OF BLACK STUDIES 1 (September 1970): 55-74.

Alexis finds that total consumption expenditures of blacks are less than for a comparable white income. Black consumers spend comparatively more for clothing and nonautomobile transportation and less for food, housing, medical care, and automobile transportation than do white consumers. There is no consistent racial difference in expenditures for either recreation and leisure or home furnishings and equipment at comparable income levels.

Caplovitz, David. THE MERCHANTS OF HARLEM: A STUDY OF SMALL BUSINESS IN A BLACK COMMUNITY. Beverly Hills, Calif.: Sage Publications, 1973. 192 p.

Caplovitz compares black and white businessmen in Harlem. Blacks had more expensive arrangements with suppliers, sought and received loans less frequently, and extended credit to customers less frequently. A major reason for these differences, according to Caplovitz, is the smaller size of black-owned businesses.

_____. THE POOR PAY MORE. New York: Free Press of Glencoe, 1963. 192 p.

Caplovitz analyzes practices of low-income families and the businesses which serve them with particular emphasis on credit availability, quality of merchandise, and prices. He concludes that the poor do pay more than whites for comparable merchandise.

Goodman, Charles S. "Do the Poor Pay More?" JOURNAL OF MARKETING 32 (January 1968): 18-24.

Goodman studied low-income residents of Philadelphia and concluded that the poor do not pay more for retail goods, because they shop out of their immediate area of residence, in localities where competitive pricing exists.

They only utilize small retail outlets with higher prices for highly perishable items.

Huber, Milton J. "The Poor in the Market Place." In POWER, POVERTY, AND URBAN POLICY. Vol. 2, pp. 151-80. Edited by Warner Bloomberg and Henry J. Schmandt. Beverly Hills, Calif.: Sage Publications, 1968.

Huber examines retailing in the ghetto. He criticizes reforms which attempt to enable ghetto residents to handle the present ghetto credit system. He advocates reform of the present system which would eliminate the ghetto merchants and the high prices and poor service they provide.

Lespare, Michael. "Hospitals and the Ghetto: A Try for Rapport." HOSPITALS 43 (July 1969): 29-33.

While major medical facilities are often located in urban ghetto areas, the two are generally unfriendly neighbors. Lespare proposes greater interaction between hospitals and their neighbors for the betterment of the health services provided to blacks.

Norman, John C., ed. MEDICINE IN THE GHETTO. New York: Appleton-Century-Crofts, 1969. 333 p.

Norman describes the quality of medical care received by ghetto residents and the operation of the medical service delivery system which keeps it at a dismal level.

Rosenblatt, Daniel. "Barriers to Medical Care for the Urban Poor." In NEW PERSPECTIVES ON POVERTY, pp. 69-76. Edited by Arthur B. Shostak and William Gomberg. Englewood Cliffs, N.J.: Prentice-Hall, 1965.

Rosenblatt focuses upon blacks and Puerto Ricans in New York City and finds that their medical care problems are largely the result of geographical inaccessibility to health care delivery systems.

Schmidt, Alvin J., and Babchuk, Nicholas. "The Unbrotherly Brotherhood: Discrimination in Fraternal Orders." PHYLON 4 (September 1973): 275-82.

Discrimination by private clubs is sanctioned by law under some circumstances and will only be removed under public pressure. The entertainment services provided by private clubs to consumers are unavailable to blacks by reason of de jure segregation.

Sengstock, Mary C. "The Corporation and the Ghetto." JOURNAL OF URBAN LAW 45 (Spring/Summer 1968): 673-703.

Sengstock examines food retailing in Detroit by comparing white middle-class areas with black residential areas. Lower priced, high volume chain stores are infrequently located in the ghetto, and ghetto residents rely upon higher priced independents. She discusses means of attracting chain stores to ghetto areas.

Sturdivant, Frederick D. "Rationality and Racism in the Ghetto Marketplace."
SOCIAL SCIENCE QUARTERLY 54 (September 1973): 380-83.

> Sturdivant finds that retail stores in ghettos charge higher prices
> than stores in the community at large. Ghetto residents do not
> have free access to other markets largely because of the need for
> credit. The reasons for the higher price of credit are unclear and
> cannot be explained rationally.

Sturdivant, Frederick D., and Hanselman, William. "Discrimination in the
Marketplace: Another Dimension." SOCIAL SCIENCE QUARTERLY 52 (December 1971): 625-30.

> An experiment in Portland, Oregon, conducted by Sturdivant and
> Hanselman demonstrated that blacks pay higher credit charges than
> whites with similar consumer credit ratings.

Sturdivant, Frederick D., and Wilhelm, Walter T. "Poverty, Minorities, and
Consumer Exploitation." SOCIAL SCIENCE QUARTERLY 49 (December 1968):
643-50.

> Sturdivant and Wilhelm tested the hypothesis that retailers outside
> the ghetto exploit minorities by charging higher finance charges.
> Through inquiries at retail establishments by minority and nonmi-
> nority persons the hypothesis was found to be true.

Chapter 8

BLACKS AND THE MANPOWER POLICIES

OF THE BUSINESS COMMUNITY

Chapter 8

BLACKS AND THE MANPOWER POLICIES
OF THE BUSINESS COMMUNITY

Abts, Henry W. "A Positive Policy." EMPLOYMENT SERVICE REVIEW 4 (March/April 1967): 10-11.

Abts describes the experience of a company which integrated its work force. He concludes that the major factor governing success is managerial attitudes. Criteria for employment that are based upon ability are the responsibility of management.

Ace, Merle E. "Psychological Testing: Unfair Discrimination." INDUSTRIAL RELATIONS 10 (October 1971): 301-15.

Ace finds that inappropriate applications of employment tests help create a large number of unemployed and underemployed people. Blacks tend to score lower than whites on most tests measuring knowledge, achievement, ability, or aptitude. The reasons for this differential include the manner in which test instructions are given, low motivation, high anxiety, and cultural bias in test content.

Adams, Arvil V[an], et al. "Plantwide Seniority, Black Employment, and Employer Affirmative Action." INDUSTRIAL AND LABOR RELATIONS REVIEW 26 (October 1972): 686-90.

The authors examine employment data at an aerospace firm during the years 1966-70 which indicate that seniority systems pose a proportionately greater burden for black workers when economic conditions worsen and layoffs occur.

Anderson, Bernard E. NEGRO EMPLOYMENT IN PUBLIC UTILITIES. Philadelphia: University of Pennsylvania Press, 1970. 261 p. Tables.

Anderson examines the racial policies of employers in the electric power, gas, and telephone industries, and presents statistics on the extent of black employment in various occupations within the industries.

111

Barnum, Donald T. THE NEGRO IN THE BITUMINOUS COAL MINING IN-
DUSTRY. Philadelphia: University of Pennsylvania Press, 1970. 65 p.
Tables.

> Barnum examines the racial policies of employers in the bituminous
> coal mining industry and presents statistics on the extent of black
> employment in various occupations within the industry.

Bell, Duran, [Jr.]. "Occupational Discrimination as a Source of Income Differences: Lessons of the 1960s." AMERICAN ECONOMIC REVIEW 62 (May 1972):
363-72. Tables.

> Bell examines the feasibility of providing subsidies to employers for
> hiring black workers.

Bloom, Gordon, F., and Fletcher, F. Marion. THE NEGRO IN THE SUPER-
MARKET INDUSTRY. Philadelphia: University of Pennsylvania Press, 1972.
314 p. Tables.

> Bloom and Fletcher examine the racial policies of employers in
> the supermarket industry and present statistics on the extent of
> black employment in various occupations within the industry.

Bloom, Gordon, F., et al. NEGRO EMPLOYMENT IN RETAIL TRADE. Philadelphia: University of Pennsylvania Press, 1972. 224 p. Tables.

> The authors examine the racial policies of employers in the depart-
> ment store, drugstore, and supermarket industries and present statis-
> tics on the extent of black employment in various occupations
> within the industries.

Blum, Albert A., and Schmidt, Charles T., Jr. "Securing Skills Needed for
Success: Community Job Training for Negroes." MANAGEMENT OF PERSON-
NEL QUARTERLY 5 (Fall 1966): 30-35.

> Blum and Schmidt outline major facets of employment training pro-
> grams for blacks.

Bows, Albert J., and Hauser, G. David. "JOBS: A Program for a Greater
Atlanta." ATLANTA ECONOMIC REVIEW 19 (May 1969): 2-3.

> The JOBS (Jobs Opportunities in the Business Sector) program is a
> subsidy from the federal government to private business for the
> operation of training programs. Bows and Hauser assess the poten-
> tial impact of the program in Atlanta, Georga.

Briggs, Vernon M., Jr. "The Negro in American Industry: A Review of Seven
Studies." JOURNAL OF HUMAN RESOURCES 5 (Summer 1970): 371-81.

> Briggs critiques studies of blacks in the automobile, aerospace,
> steel, hotel, petroleum, rubber, and chemical industries conducted

by the Industrial Research Unit, Wharton School of Finance and Commerce, University of Pennsylvania, in "The Racial Policies of American Industries" series.

"Building Up Minority Contractors." MANPOWER 1 (October 1969): 23-25.

The article describes a program to train blacks as construction contractors.

Callender, Eugene S. "Business and the Hard-Core Unemployed: The Ghetto Subculture." PERSONNEL 45 (July/August 1968): 8-14.

Callender describes efforts business should expend in order to increase the employment of the black hard-core unemployed.

Carter, Leonard. "Corporate Apartheid." CENTER MAGAZINE 5 (January/ February 1971): 71-73.

Carter finds that blacks and Mexican-Americans are absent from the boards of directors and executive ranks of the sixty-seven largest corporations headquartered in California. Because the corporations receive government subsidies, legal action appears to be the most feasibile means for improvement.

Cohn, Jules. "The New Business of Business--A Study of a Corporate Program for the Disadvantaged." URBAN AFFAIRS QUARTERLY 6 (September 1970): 71-87.

Cohn observes that the key problem for employers in training unemployed minority workers is the need to balance the goals of running a profitable business and providing the needs of the workers.

Corwin, R. David. "Occupational Mobility and Minority Workers--A Case Study." URBAN AFFAIRS QUARTERLY 6 (September 1970): 41-51.

Corwin finds that minority workers are concentrated in lower echelon jobs in the banking industry. The general assumption has been that within a relatively short period of time the regular promotion processes would result in a normal distribution of minority workers in the occupational hierarchy. This assumption is unwarranted due to formal and informal promotion criteria which tend to place minorities at a disadvantage.

Culhane, Margaret M. "Testing the Disadvantaged." EMPLOYMENT SERVICE REVIEW 2 (May 1965): 8-9.

The problem of testing culturally disadvantaged employment applicants arises from the development of norms based upon a nonculturally disadvantaged test group.

Dizard, Jan E. "Why Should Negroes Work?" In NEGROES AND JOBS, pp. 400-414. Edited by Louis A. Ferman et al. Ann Arbor: University of Michigan Press, 1968.

> According to Dizard, blacks, like whites, desire a decent job, education, home, and all the other things they have so long been deprived of, but it may be wrong to assume that they are committed to obtaining these goals by the same means as whites. To the extent that blacks do not aspire to upward occupational mobility, a job is only valuable for the money it pays now. Therefore, Dizard concludes that manpower training programs may continue to suffer from low retention rates.

Ferman, Louis A. THE NEGRO AND EQUAL EMPLOYMENT OPPORTUNITIES. New York: Frederick A. Praeger, Publishers, 1968. 195 p. Tables.

> Ferman examines the equal employment efforts of twenty business firms. The obstacles to improvement include a shortage of skilled black workers, priority of work standards over equal employment opportunity by management, resistance to special training programs by management, and resistance by unions to modifications in seniority and apprenticeship practices. Employers were generally found to be satisfied with the performance of black workers. White workers resist the concept of preferential treatment, and blacks qualified for higher paying jobs often fail to apply.

Fletcher, F. Marion. THE NEGRO IN THE DRUG MANUFACTURING INDUSTRY. Philadelphia: University of Pennsylvania Press, 1970. 109 p. Tables.

> Fletcher examines the racial policies of employers in the drug manufacturing industry and presents statistics on the extent of black employment in various occupations within the industry.

_____. THE NEGRO IN THE DRUGSTORE INDUSTRY. Philadelphia: University of Pennsylvania Press, 1971. 131 p. Tables.

> Fletcher examines the racial policies of employers in the drugstore industry and presents statistics on the extent of black employment in various occupations within the industry.

Fletcher, Linda P[ickthorne]. THE NEGRO IN THE INSURANCE INDUSTRY. Philadelphia: University of Pennsylvania Press, 1970. 173 p. Tables.

> Fletcher examines the racial policies of employment in the insurance industry and presents statistics on the extent of black employment in various occupations within the industry.

Fogel, Walter [A.]. "Blacks in Meatpacking: Another View of the Jungle." INDUSTRIAL RELATIONS 10 (October 1971): 338-53.

Fogel traces the development of race relations in meatpacking during this century.

_____. "Labor Market Obstacles to Minority Job Gains." In THE DEVELOP-MENT AND USE OF MANPOWER, pp. 97-104. Edited by Gerald G. Somers. Madison, Wis.: Industrial Relations Research Association, 1967.

Among the obstacles to the hiring and promotion of minorities are education and skill requirements which often have little to do with productivity. According to Fogel, changes in the selection process are necessary.

_____. THE NEGRO IN THE MEAT INDUSTRY. Philadelphia: University of Pennsylvania Press, 1970. 124 p. Tables.

Fogel examines the racial policies of employers and unions in the meat industry and presents statistics on the extent of black employment in various occupations within the industry.

French, Robert L. "The Motorola Case." THE INDUSTRIAL PSYCHOLOGIST 2 (August 1965): 29-50. Tables.

This case before the Illinois Fair Employment Practices Commission prompted Congress to include a provision in the 1964 Civil Rights Act which prohibits challenges to employment tests on the basis that the type of exam is inherently discriminatory against minorities. The Illinois Commission ruled that Motorola discriminated against a black on that basis. French discusses the difficulties in developing employment tests which do not contain cultural bias.

Fulmer, William E. THE NEGRO IN THE FURNITURE INDUSTRY. Philadelphia: University of Pennsylvania Press, 1972. 207 p. Tables.

Fulmer examines the racial policies of employers in the furniture industry and presents statistics on the extent of black employment in various occupations within the industry.

Gershenfeld, Walter J. "An Insight into Structural Unemployment--The Experience of a Minority Group in a Prosperous Community." ECONOMIC AND BUSINESS BULLETIN 18 (1965): 1-7.

In the midst of full employment of whites in a geographic area, black unemployment is high and in the nature of structural unemployment, which can be dealt with through retraining.

Greene, Lorenzo J., and Woodson, Carter W. THE NEGRO WAGE EARNER. Washington, D.C.: Association for the Study of Negro Life and History, 1930. 189 p.

This is a classic study of the obstacles confronted by black labor after the Civil War. Based to a large extent upon interviews with black workers, it provides a valuable historical perspective.

Guion, Robert M. "Employment Tests and Discriminatory Hiring." In NEGROES AND JOBS, pp. 323–28. Edited by Louis A. Ferman et al. Ann Arbor: University of Michigan Press, 1968. Tables.

> Guion finds that most companies using psychological tests in their employment procedures do not use them competently. Tests are used with no knowledge of their validities for a particular situation. Any competent psychologist can develop tests which discriminate in illegal ways. Guion suggests types of research which should be conducted in order to validate examinations.

Habbe, Stephen. "Recruiting Negro College Graduates." THE CONFERENCE BOARD 8 (August 1964): 7–9.

> A survey by Habbe of forty large companies prior to the passage of the 1964 Civil Rights Act disclosed that 80 percent recruited graduates of Negro colleges.

Harlem Youth Opportunities Unlimited. "Barriers to Parity in Employment." In NEGROES AND JOBS, pp. 239–48. Edited by Louis A. Ferman et al. Ann Arbor: University of Michigan Press, 1968.

> While entry into many jobs is controlled by a series of requirements which are guides to the skills needed to enter the job, for black applicants these guides become a rigid set of qualifications. According to this report failure to meet even one requirement is a ground for rejection.

Harrison, Bennett. "Human Capital, Black Poverty, and 'Radical' Economics." INDUSTRIAL RELATIONS 10 (October 1971): 277–86.

> By reviewing literature supporting a contrary view, Harrison disputes the contention that "radical" economists support manpower training programs for blacks in order to reduce black poverty. Discriminatory white institutions must be restructured and new black institu0 tions built.

Hefner, James A., and Kidder, Alice E. [Handsaker]. "Racial Integration in Southern Management Positions." PHYLON 33 (Summer 1972): 193–200.

> Hefner and Kidder find that despite some breakthroughs, blacks are vastly underrepresented in management positions at southern firms. The reasons cited are discrimination, little federal government contracting by many southern firms, and the movement of graduates from black southern colleges to the North.

Henderson, Vivian W. "Manpower Development and Equal Employment Opportuntiy." In MANPOWER POLICY: PERSPECTIVES AND PROSPECTS, pp. 89–98. Edited by Seymour L. Wolfbein. Philadelphia: Temple University School of Business Administration, 1973.

Henderson observes that manpower programs often train blacks for dead-end jobs or jobs with irregular employment. She proposes greater coordination between manpower and equal opportunity policies, and cooperation from the business community.

Herbst, Alma. THE NEGRO IN THE SLAUGHTERING AND MEAT PACKING INDUSTRY IN CHICAGO. New York: Houghton Mifflin Co., 1932. 182 p.

This is a classic study of foreign immigration and black migration into an industry through a chain of strike clashes, the efforts of employers to foster racial and ethnic hatred, and the maintenance of the conditions described in Sinclair's THE JUNGLE.

Hill, Herbert. "Employment, Manpower Training and the Black Worker." JOURNAL OF NEGRO EDUCATION 38 (Summer 1969): 204-17.

Hill observes that blacks are concentrated in jobs with declining employment prospects for the future. Government sponsored manpower training programs maintain traditional occupational patterns for blacks, while state employment services do not provide information on nontraditional jobs. Housing segregation prevents blacks from gaining access to jobs in expanding suburban industrial areas.

_____. "Racial Inequality in Employment: The Patterns of Discrimination." ANNALS OF THE AMERICAN ACADEMY OF POLITICAL AND SOCIAL SCIENCE 357 (January 1965): 39-47.

Hill, Joseph. "Steel: Changing Workplace." DISSENT 19 (Winter 1972): 37-46.

Hill chronicles the relegation of blacks to the most undesirable jobs at a steel plant.

Hill, Norman. "Which Jobs for the Blacks?" NEW GENERATION 50 (Winter 1968): 7-10.

Hill describes the exclusion of blacks from white-collar and managerial jobs, particularly in the airline, banking, insurance, medical, securities, and utility industries.

Hjornevik, Wesley L. "Manpower Policy--An Instrument of Social Change: Equal Employment, Welfare, Poverty." In MANPOWER POLICY: PERSPECTIVES AND PROSPECTS, pp. 109-15. By Seymour L. Wolfbein. Philadelphia: Temple University School of Business Administration, 1973.

Hjornevik finds that the manpower policy in the United States has concentrated on the characteristics of the labor force and has not been coordinated nor used in conjunction with policies to increase the demand for labor. This, Hjornevik concludes, is a major reason why the goal of equal employment has not been attained.

Holmes, Adolph. "Urban League Upgrades Negro Workers." EMPLOYMENT SERVICE REVIEW 3 (August 1966): 25-28.

> Holmes describes the efforts of a private civil rights organization, in cooperation with the business sector, to improve the employment of black workers.

Howard, John C. THE NEGRO IN THE LUMBER INDUSTRY. Philadelphia: University of Pennsylvania Press, 1970. 76 p. Tables.

> Howard examines the racial policies of employers in the lumber industry and presents statistics on the extent of black employment in various occupations within the industry.

Institute for Social Research, University of Michigan. DISCRIMINATION WITHOUT PREJUDICE: A STUDY OF PROMOTION PRACTICES IN INDUSTRY. Ann Arbor: Survey Research Center, University of Michigan, 1964. 46 p. Tables and charts.

> Companies with "equal opportunity policies" promote few minority group members into managerial ranks. Promotion criteria such as leadership, personality, and motivation are far from objective. Decision makers generally follow what they believe will be most acceptable to fellow managers, their superiors, customers, and employees supervised by the party to be promoted. Ability to perform the job, states this report, should be the only criterion for promotion, and "ability" should be defined in specific, objective terms.

Institute of Labor and Industrial Relations, University of Michigan--Wayne State University. "A Study of Patterns of Discrimination in Employment." 1966. Mimeograph.

> State and city equal employment opportunity commissions were found to be more concerned with adjudicating complaints by individuals than with investigating and eliminating patterns of discrimination. Employers have not changed discriminatory practices despite the existence of laws.

Jeffress, Philip W. THE NEGRO IN THE URBAN TRANSIT INDUSTRY. Philadelphia: University of Pennsylvania Press, 1970. 106 p. Tables.

> Jeffress examines the racial policies of employers and unions in the urban transit industry and presents statistics on the extent of black employment in various occupations within the industry.

Johnson, Fred R. "Recruiting, Retraining, and Advancing Minority Employees." TRAINING AND DEVELOPMENT JOURNAL 26 (January 1972): 28-31.

> The employment of minorities in nontraditional occupations is fraught with many problems for both the employer and the new employee. Johnson enumerates techniques for overcoming these obstacles.

Kidder, David E., and Kidder, Alice E. [Handsaker]. "Reflections on 'Black Economics.'" GROWTH AND CHANGE 1 (April 1970): 11-16.

> Classical economic theory does not allow for the pervasive economic inequality that exists between blacks and whites. According to the Kidders, theories of group behavior are perhaps more appropriate than the individualistic classical theory.

King, Carl B., and Risher, Howard W. THE NEGRO IN THE PETROLEUM INDUSTRY. Philadelphia: University of Pennsylvania Press, 1969. 96 p. Tables.

> King and Risher examine the racial policies of employers in the petroleum industry and present data on the extent of black employment in various occupations within the industry.

Kirkpatrick, James J. TESTING AND FAIR EMPLOYMENT: FAIRNESS AND VALIDITY OF PERSONNEL TESTS FOR DIFFERENT ETHNIC GROUPS. New York: New York University Press, 1968. 145 p. Tables.

> Kirkpatrick advocates the use of different employment tests for different ethnic groups, which is contrary to fair employment laws. Tests which are useful in predicting job success for one ethnic group are not always useful for other ethnic groups. He suggests certain improvements in the accuracy of predictive devices.

Koziara, Edward C., and Koziara, Karen S. THE NEGRO IN THE HOTEL INDUSTRY. Philadelphia: University of Pennsylvania Press, 1968. 74 p. Tables.

> The Koziaras examine the racial policies of employers in the hotel industry and present data on the extent of black employment in various occupations within the industry.

Leone, Richard D. THE NEGRO IN THE TRUCKING INDUSTRY. Philadelphia: University of Pennsylvania Press, 1970. 132 p. Tables.

> Leone examines the racial policies of employers and unions in the trucking industry and presents statistics on the extent of black employment in various occupations within the industry.

Levitan, Sar [A.], and Siegel, Irving H. DIMENSIONS OF MANPOWER POLICY: PROGRAMS AND RESEARCH. Baltimore: Johns Hopkins Press, 1966. 299 p. Tables.

> Levitan and Siegel examine the Manpower Development and Training Act, Youth Employment Act, and Economic Opportunity Act, which are designed to affect structural unemployment, particularly among minorities.

Levitan, Sar A., et al. ECONOMIC OPPORTUNITY IN THE GHETTO: THE PARTNERSHIP OF GOVERNMENT AND BUSINESS. Baltimore: Johns Hopkins

Press, 1970. 84 p.

> Programs to open existing jobs to ghetto residents are more efficient
> than efforts to create new jobs for ghetto residents or programs to
> foster minority-owned businesses. Manpower training programs and
> improved education are the best means for improving the employ-
> ability of ghetto residents.

Lipsky, David B., and Rose, Joseph B. "Craft Entry for Minorities: The Case
of Project Justice." INDUSTRIAL RELATIONS 10 (October 1971): 301-15.
Tables.

> Lipsky and Rose describe a project to train blacks to become
> journeymen in Buffalo, New York. Half the trainees qualified
> to become building tradesmen. Admittance had little relationship
> to education, work experience, and training.

Lockwood, Howard C. "Critical Problems in Achieving Equal Employment Opportunity." EMPLOYMENT SERVICE REVIEW 3 (August 1966): 14-17.

> The effects of discrimination in the past make the addition of the
> phrase "equal opportunity employer" to newspaper advertisements
> and corporate letterheads ineffective. Lockwood describes recruit-
> ment and training efforts which can overcome the effects of past
> discrimination.

Mangum, Garth L. MDTA FOUNDATIONS OF FEDERAL MANPOWER POLICY.
Baltimore: Johns Hopkins Press, 1968. 184 p. Tables.

> Mangum analyzes the intent and effectiveness of the Manpower
> Development and Training Act with particular emphasis on minorities.
> His basic conclusion is that while participation of nonwhites in
> MDTA programs has increased and those who have received assistance
> are generally better situated, the scope of the programs has been
> too limited to affect the economic condition of the structurally un-
> employed and underemployed.

Marshall, Patricia. "Testing without Reading." MANPOWER 3 (May 1971):
7-12.

> Marshall describes a test which measures a person's vocational
> aptitude regardless of his education or experience.

Marshall, [F.] Ray. "Racial Factors Influencing Entry into the Skilled Trades."
In HUMAN RESOURCES IN THE URBAN ECONOMY, pp. 18-32. Edited by
Mark Perlman. Baltimore: Johns Hopkins Press, 1963.

> Marshall finds that the factors preventing black entrance into the
> skilled trades are easy identification, the image of inferiority
> fostered by slavery and popular white culture, and the feeling of
> superiority by workers in lily-white occupations, which in their
> view are downgraded by the inclusion of blacks. Living in segre-
> gated neighborhoods, blacks seldom hear about training and job

opportunities in skilled occupations.

_____. "Reflections on Upgrading." MANPOWER 2 (January 1970): 2-7.

Marshall observes that only very tight labor market conditions will
lead to training programs conducted by businesses which will result
in job upgrading for blacks and other minorities.

_____. "The Employment and Training of Minorities." In CHALLENGES TO
COLLECTIVE BARGAINING, pp. 89-112. Edited by Lloyd Ulman. Englewood
Cliffs, N.J.: Prentice-Hall, 1967.

Marshall observes that to the employer and the economist, the
difference between training and preferential treatment is the difference between making black workers worth more and paying them
more than they are worth. To white workers the difference is
not so clear. According to Marshall, full employment is a prerequisite for the success of both training and preferential treatment.

Miller, Brian P. "IQ Tests and Minority Groups." TRAINING AND DEVELOP-
MENT JOURNAL 25 (October 1971): 26-27.

While IQ tests are not supposed to reflect educational exposure,
an experiment conducted by Miller indicates that they do. Blacks
and other minorities are hampered by this failure of the testing
and placement process to differentiate innate and environmental
factors.

Mitchell, Bobby. "Pro Sports: Road to Riches or Dead End?" MANPOWER
3 (December 1971): 15-21.

Pro sports reward a few blacks who compete in athletics. The
majority, however, do not succeed; and those who do find opportunities after retirement from sports limited.

Mogull, Robert G. "Discrimination in the Labor Market." JOURNAL OF
BLACK STUDIES 3 (December 1972): 237-49.

Mogull finds that by reducing wage discrimination against women
and blacks the result will be a decline in employment opportunities.
This has been the case in the South, where wages have become
standardized between blacks and whites. Discrimination against
women by employers appears to have been increasing in recent
years, and the relative economic improvement for black men has
been slow. Mogull hypothesizes that reducing wage discrimination
against women will probably be at the expense of black men.

Mulligan, James H. "Talent Search Challenges Chicago's Street Gangs."
IDEA 1 (November 1969): 1-5.

National Advisory Commission on Civil Disorders. SUPPLEMENTAL STUDIES

FOR THE NATIONAL ADVISORY COMMISSION ON CIVIL DISORDERS. New York: Frederick A. Praeger, Publishers, 1968. 248 p. Tables.

This supplement to the Kerner Commission Report contains studies commissioned by the group analyzing the ghetto riots of the 1960s and upon which the final report was written. Of special interest are studies of "Major Employers and Their Manpower Policies" and "Doing Business in the Ghetto: Retail Merchants." Both contain the perceptions of white employers toward blacks.

Nickeson, Steve. "EEOC Criticizes Ma Bell's Hiring." RACE RELATIONS REPORTER 3 (January 17, 1972): 6-8.

Nickeson enumerates the extent of minority participation in the Bell telephone system.

Northrup, Herbert R. "In-Plant Movement of Negroes in the Aerospace Industry." MONTHLY LABOR REVIEW 91 (February 1968): 22-25.

Among the obstacles to an improved employment situation for blacks in the aerospace industry are a lack of skill and a lack of access to jobs located outside inner cities. Blacks are harder hit by layoffs than whites due to lower seniority, and they are often not motivated to participate in training programs. Arrest records, however, are not an automatic bar to employment as in the past.

_____. THE NEGRO IN THE AEROSPACE INDUSTRY. Philadelphia: University of Pennsylvania Press, 1968. 90 p. Tables.

Northrup examines the racial policies of employers in the aerospace industry and presents data on the extent of black employment in various occupations within the industry.

_____. THE NEGRO IN THE AUTOMOBILE INDUSTRY. Philadelphia: University of Pennsylvania Press, 1968. 75 p. Tables.

Northrup traces the development of black employment in the auto industry. Black job upgrading has been greatest when shortages of white workers exist. Increasingly, unskilled and semiskilled jobs in the industry are being dominated by blacks, while black movement into skilled jobs is minimal.

_____. THE NEGRO IN THE PAPER INDUSTRY. Philadelphia: University of Pennsylvania Press, 1969. 233 p. Tables.

Northrup examines the racial policies of employers in the paper industry and presents statistics on the extent of black employment in various occupations within the industry.

_____. THE NEGRO IN THE TOBACCO INDUSTRY. Philadelphia: University of Pennsylvania Press, 1970. 92 p. Tables.

Northrup examines the racial policies of employers in the tobacco

industry and presents statistics on the extent of black employment
in various occupations within the industry.

Northrup, Herbert R., and Batchelder, Alan B. THE NEGRO IN THE RUBBER
TIRE INDUSTRY. Philadelphia: University of Pennsylvania Press, 1969. 134 p.
Tables.

Northrup and Batchelder examine the racial policies of employers
in the rubber tire industry and present data on the extent of black
employment in various occupations within the industry.

Northrup, Herbert R., et al. NEGRO EMPLOYMENT IN BASIC INDUSTRY.
Philadelphia: University of Pennsylvania Press, 1970. 769 p. Tables.

The authors present data on the total black employment and occupational distribution in the automobile, aerospace, steel, rubber
tire, petroleum, and chemical industries. Hiring and promotion
policies are described and compared between industries. Blacks
have made their greatest employment gains in times of relatively
full employment. The authors examine the effect of labor market
conditions on employment in industries, the effect of having employed blacks in traditional occupations, and the relation of racial
employment policies with the degree of consumer market orientation.

_____. NEGRO EMPLOYMENT IN LAND AND AIR TRANSPORT. Philadel-
phia: University of Pennsylvania Press, 1971. Var. pag. Tables.

The authors examine the racial policies of employers and unions in
the railroad, airline, trucking, and urban transit industries and
present statistics on the extent of black employment in various
occupations within the industries.

_____. NEGRO EMPLOYMENT IN SOUTHERN INDUSTRY. Philadelphia:
University of Pennsylvania Press, 1970. Var. pag. Tables.

The authors examine the racial policies of employers in the paper,
lumber, tobacco, coal mining, and textile industries and present
statistics on the extent of black employment in various occupations
within the industries.

_____. THE NEGRO IN THE AIR TRANSPORT INDUSTRY. Philadelphia:
University of Pennsylvania Press, 1971. 146 p. Tables.

The authors examine the racial policies of employers in the air
transport industry and present statistics on the extent of black
employment in various occupations within the industry.

Odell, Charles. "Training the Disadvantaged, Using All Our Resources." In
TECHNICAL TRAINING FOR THE DISADVANTAGED, pp. 6-10. By U.S.
Department of Labor, Management Administration. Washington, D.C.: 1969.

Odell describes a program to train the disadvantaged for technical

positions, sponsored jointly by private business and government.
Lower labor costs were incurred by the company as a result of the
subsidization.

Oliva, Max. "Selection Techniques and the Black Hard-Core Male." PERSON-
NEL JOURNAL 49 (May 1970): 424-30.

According to Oliva, the employment application and interview
must be modified to fit the capabilities of the hard-core unemployed. The author fails to examine the possibility of altering
the employment characteristics of the hard-core unemployed so as
to improve their accessibility to employers.

Osburn, Donald D. NEGRO EMPLOYMENT IN THE TEXTILE INDUSTRIES OF
NORTH AND SOUTH CAROLINA. Washington, D.C.: Equal Employment
Opportunity Commission, 1966. 58 p. Tables. Sold by Government Printing
Office.

Foreign competition and the resultant need for technological change
have altered the types and number of jobs in the textile industry.
The position of blacks within this changing labor market is not improving. Improved education and affirmative action by employers
is necessary if blacks are even to retain their existing position
within the industry.

Ozanne, Robert. THE NEGRO IN THE FARM EQUIPMENT AND CONSTRUC-
TION MACHINERY INDUSTRY. Philadelphia: University of Pennsylvania Press,
1972. 115 p. Tables.

Ozanne examines the racial policies of employers and unions in
the farm equipment and construction machinery industry and presents statistics on the extent of black employment in various occupations within the industry.

Patten, Thomas H., and Clark, Gerald E. "Literary Training and Job Placement of Hard-Core Unemployed Negroes in Detroit." JOURNAL OF HUMAN
RESOURCES 3 (Winter 1968): 25-46.

Patten and Clark tested the relative effectiveness of two approaches
to reading among hard-core, functionally illiterate, unemployed
blacks. One year after the program, few were employed. According to the authors, the achievement of literacy and job placement
remain difficult for the hard-core unemployed.

Pearl, Arthur. "Education, Employment, and Civil Rights for Negro Youth."
In POVERTY, EDUCATION, AND RACE RELATIONS: STUDIES AND PRO-
POSALS, pp. 49-60. Edited by William C. Kovaraceus, John S. Gibson, and
Thomas J. Curtin. Boston: Allyn and Bacon, 1967.

_____. "The Poverty of Psychology--An Indictment." In PSYCHOLOGICAL
FACTORS IN POVERTY, pp. 348-364. Edited by Vernon L. Allen. Chicago:

Markham Publishing Co., 1970.

> Pearl identifies education and test performance "credentials" as a major obstacle to improved employment for the poor. He charges psychologists with the task of developing predictive measures of job performance which are not biased toward the lower socioeconomic classes and racial and ethnic minorities.

Perry, Charles R. THE NEGRO IN THE DEPARTMENT STORE INDUSTRY. Philadelphia: University of Pennsylvania Press, 1971. 155 p. Tables.

> Perry examines the racial policies of employers in the department store industry and presents statistics on the extent of black employment in various occupations in the industry.

Petshek, Kirk R. "Barriers to Employability of Negroes in White-Collar Jobs." In THE DEVELOPMENT AND USE OF MANPOWER, pp. 105-11. Edited by Gerald G. Somers. Madison, Wis.: Industrial Relations Research Association, 1967.

> Interpersonal relationships are more important in white-collar than in blue-collar employment. Petshek suggests that the prime obstacle to greater black employment in white-collar jobs may be white employer and employee prejudice over interpersonal relations with blacks.

Purcell, Theodore V., and Cavanagh, Gerald F. BLACKS IN THE INDUSTRIAL WORLD: ISSUES FOR THE MANAGER. New York: Free Press, 1972. 232 p.

> Purcell and Cavanagh observe that in order to implement an equal employment policy, businesses should follow a systems approach of locating responsibility, communicating policy, identifying problem areas, establishing goals and timetables, developing programs to meet targets, and evaluating effectiveness.

Purcell, Theodore V., and Mulvey, Daniel P. THE NEGRO IN THE ELECTRICAL MANUFACTURING INDUSTRY. Philadelphia: University of Pennsylvania Press, 1971. 146 p. Tables.

> Purcell and Mulvey examine the racial policies of employers in the electrical manufacturing industry and present statistics on the extent of black employment in various occupations within the industry.

Quay, William Howard. THE NEGRO IN THE CHEMICAL INDUSTRY. Philadelphia: University of Pennsylvania Press, 1969. 110 p. Tables.

> Quay examines the racial policies of employers in the chemical industry and presents statistics on the extent of black employment in various occupations within the industry.

Rafky, David M. "The Black Scholar in the Academic Marketplace." TEACHERS COLLEGE RECORD 74 (December 1972): 224-60.

Rafky describes the educational and familial characteristics of black college teachers and the types of schools hiring them. He speculates on the reasons why predominantly white colleges have not hired more black scholars. These factors include competition with black colleges and bottlenecks in job market information channels.

Riessman, Frank, et al. "Upgrading--The Next Priority in Manpower Policy." URBAN AFFAIRS QUARTERLY 6 (September 1970): 33-40.

Manpower programs to provide opportunities for upgrading low-skilled workers are a relatively recent phenomenon encouraged by government subsidy programs. The authors review one employer's upgrading program.

Risher, Howard W. THE NEGRO IN THE RAILROAD INDUSTRY. Philadelphia: University of Pennsylvania Press, 1971. 202 p. Tables.

Risher examines the racial policies of employers and unions in the railroad industry and presents statistics on the extent of black employment in various occupations within the industry.

Rosen, Doris B. EMPLOYMENT TESTING AND MINORITY GROUPS, AS REPORTED IN THE LITERATURE. Ithaca, N.Y.: Cornell University, School of Industrial and Labor Relations, 1970. 30 p.

This is an excellent review article of employment testing and its effects upon minorities.

Rosen, Ned A., et al. "Personnal Testing and Equal Opportunity." ILR RESEARCH 13 (November 1967): 19-23.

Rosenberg, Bernard, and Howton, F. William. "Ethnic Liberalism and Employment Discrimination in the North." AMERICAN JOURNAL OF ECONOMICS AND SOCIOLOGY 26 (October 1967): 387-98.

Rosenberg and Howton find that northern employers generally deny that discrimination is the cause of the lower occupational status of blacks. Despite these denials, blacks are viewed as unsuited for skilled work. Within the firms that the author studied, whites were preferentially hired and upgraded in both blue-collar and white-collar jobs. They contend that employers are ready for change, but the government will have to be more aggressive in compelling equal employment opportunity.

Rowan, Richard L. "Negro Employment in the Basic Steel Industry." INDUSTRIAL AND LABOR RELATIONS REVIEW 23 (October 1969): 29-39.

An examination of the extent of black employment in the basic steel industry reveals that there has been a small but encouraging gain in the share of jobs held by blacks in all occupational categories except sales. The largest percentage of increase in black employees has been in the technician and clerical groups, but participation in white-collar jobs is low as compared to blue-collar jobs. However, the outlook for increased black employment in white-collar positions is encouraging.

_____. THE NEGRO IN THE STEEL INDUSTRY. Philadelphia: University of Pennsylvania Press, 1968. 148 p. Tables.

Rowan examines the racial policies of employers in the steel industry and presents data on the extent of black employment in various occupations within the industry.

_____. THE NEGRO IN THE TEXTILE INDUSTRY. Philadelphia: University of Pennsylvania Press, 1970. 172 p. Tables.

Rowan examines the racial policies of employers in the textile industry and presents statistics on the extent of black employment in various occupations within the industry.

_____. "A Review of Research on the Negro and Employment in the South." ECONOMIC AND BUSINESS BULLETIN 17 (March 1965): 20-31.

This is an out-of-date yet valuable review of black employment in the South.

Rubin, Lester. THE NEGRO IN THE SHIPBUILDING INDUSTRY. Philadelphia: University of Pennsylvania Press, 1970. 154 p. Tables.

Rubin examines the racial policies of employers in the shipbuilding industry and presents statistics on the extent of black employment in various occupations within the industry.

Sarratt, John L. "Arrest Records as a Racially Discriminatory Employment Criterion: Gregory V. Litton Systems, Inc." (C.D. Cal. 1970). HARVARD CIVIL RIGHTS--CIVIL LIBERTIES LAW REVIEW 6 (December 1970): 165-78.

Although arrest records are not used as a hiring criterion by the federal government, some employers still do use them. According to Sarratt, blacks are subject to arrest more than whites and use of this criterion is discriminatory.

Schrank, Robert, and Stein, Susan. "IBM in the Ghetto: Anatomy of a Success." MANPOWER 4 (May 1972): 23-26.

Schrank and Stein describe the operation of an IBM manufacturing plant located in a ghetto since 1968. Employee productivity and attendance are on a par with other IBM plants. Obstacles to further ghetto expansion are the cost and time of acquiring land and the two to three years waiting time required for the enterprise to become self-sustaining. IBM hired workers on the basis of previous experience and did not administer tests.

Seligson, Harry. "Minority Group Employees, Discipline and the Arbitrator."

LABOR LAW JOURNAL 19 (September 1968): 544-54.

> Seligson examines the criteria upon which employers are allowed
> to discipline employees. He concludes that these criteria are in-
> valid when evaluating hard-core unemployed minority group workers.

Shepherd, William G., and Levin, Sharon G. "Managerial Discrimination in
Large Firms." REVIEW OF ECONOMICS AND STATISTICS 55 (November 1973):
412-22. Tables.

> Shepherd and Levin find that blacks are represented in token num-
> bers in the managerial ranks of large firms. Attempts to predict
> what factors account for even this number fail. The known sources
> of further opportunity are few and weak.

Shlensky, Bertram C. "Determinants of Turnover in Training Programs for the
Disadvantaged." PERSONNEL ADMINISTRATION 35 (March/April 1972): 53-
61.

Simpson, George S. "Employment Policy Problems in a Multiracial Society."
JOURNAL OF HUMAN RELATIONS 11 (Autumn 1962): 43.

> Simpson finds that hiring policies of employers reflect the prejudices,
> anxieties, and hostilities of the community at large. Even without
> the support of the dominant group, a minority can reverse discrim-
> ination in employment through concerted action which is disruptive
> to the majority.

Sowell, Thomas. "Race and the Market." REVIEW OF BLACK POLITICAL
ECONOMY 3 (Summer 1973): 1-25.

> Sowell theorizes that the cost of maintaining discrimination is much
> higher to profit-maximizing firms in competitive markets than to
> nonprofit firms. When political pressure is introduced, profit-maxi-
> mizing firms are the first to accede.

Strauss, George, and Ingerman, Sidney. "Vocational Education for Negro
Youth." In NEGROES AND JOBS, pp. 212-21. Edited by Louis A. Ferman
et al. Ann Arbor: University of Michigan Press, 1968.

> Strauss and Ingerman find that the evidence does not suggest voca-
> tional education should be eliminated, but it should be improved.
> Less emphasis should be placed on training for specific jobs. More
> emphasis should be placed on English and mathematics. Second-
> class status of vocational education should be eliminated by estab-
> lishing comprehensive high schools. Cooperative part-time work
> programs should be established, according to the authors, in order
> to prepare black youth to meet the skill requirements of employers.

Strauss, Robert P. "Industrial Patterns of Male Negro Employment." JOURNAL
OF HUMAN RESOURCES 7 (Winter 1972): 111-18. Tables.

Strauss examines the industrial distribution of male Negro employment in 1960. His examination indicates that an industry tends to
hire Negroes in all occupations or not at all. Generally, blacks
are underrepresented in the higher-paying occupations. Because
of the prevalence of discrimination in employment, the provision
of more and better education for blacks will not necessarily improve
their job opportunities.

Thieblot, Armand J., Jr. THE NEGRO IN THE BANKING INDUSTRY. Philadelphia: University of Pennsylvania Press, 1970. 211 p. Tables.

Thieblot examines the racial policies of employers in the banking
industry and presents statistics on the extent of black employment
in various occupations within the industry.

Thieblot, Armand J., Jr., and Fletcher, Linda Pickthorne. NEGRO EMPLOY-
MENT IN FINANCE. Philadelphia: University of Pennsylvania Press, 1970.
198 p. Tables.

Thieblot and Fletcher examine the racial policies of employers in
the banking and insurance industries and present statistics on the
extent of black employment in various occupations within the industry.

Trooboff, Benjamin. "Employment Opportunities for Negroes in the Health Related Occupations." JOURNAL OF NEGRO EDUCATION 38 (Winter 1969):
22-31.

Trooboff finds that opportunities for blacks in health related occupations abound. The major reason for underrepresentation is inadequate educational attainment. He recommends an overhaul of the
medical training system.

Weston, Zack J. "Showing the Way in Preparing Negro Jobseekers." EM-
PLOYMENT SERVICE REVIEW 3 (August 1966): 45-47.

Weston describes a successful training program in South Carolina.
The biggest obstacle was to convince trainees that work would be
available upon the completion of training. The cooperation of the
business community is a requisite for successful manpower programs.

Wiener, Rose. "Does Everybody Need a High School Diploma?" MANPOWER
1 (February/March 1969): 7-9.

Wiener advocates a reexamination of employment criteria which
exclude minority group workers but are unnecessary for job performance.

Wolters, Raymond. "The Negro in American Industries." INDUSTRIAL AND
LABOR RELATIONS REVIEW 25 (October 1971): 116-23.

Wolters traces an improved employment condition for blacks during the 1960s which is closely correlated with economic expansion and government equal employment pressure. The source of these observations is a review of sixteen out of thirty-one of "The Racial Policies of American Industry" series, produced by the Industrial Research Unit, Wharton School of Finance and Commerce, University of Pennsylvania.

Yetman, Norman, and Eitzen, D. Stanley. "Black Americans in Sports: Unequal Opportunity for Equal Ability." CIVIL RIGHTS DIGEST 5 (August 1972): 21-34.

Yetman and Eitzen find that blacks are underrepresented in leadership roles in American sports and must perform better than whites in order to play.

Young, Whitney. "Integration in Industry." FACTORY 122 (December 1964): 49-54.

Based upon a survey of industry experiences, a major factor contributing to the black's low economic position is a lack of skill. Where hired or promoted into nontraditional jobs, the basis for promotion has been ability; little opposition has been expressed by white customers and employees, even though performances have been equal to that of whites.

Zimpel, Lloyd, and Panger, Daniel. BUSINESS AND THE HARDCORE UNEMPLOYED. New York: Frederick Fell, 1970. 275 p. Tables.

Zimpel and Panger blueprint methods for business to recruit, train, and utilize the hard-core unemployed.

Chapter 9

BLACKS AND THE LABOR MOVEMENT

Chapter 9

BLACKS AND THE LABOR MOVEMENT

Ashenfelter, Orley. "Racial Discrimination and Trade Unionism." JOURNAL OF POLITICAL ECONOMY 80 (May/June 1972): 435-64. Tables.

> Ashenfelter finds that whether trade unions increase or decrease, the extent of labor market discrimination against black workers depends upon the size of the union-nonunion wage differential in the industry as well as the extent to which the industry's labor force is unionized. The 1967 ratio of black to white male wages was 4 percent higher in the industrial union sector and 5 percent lower in the craft union sector.

Brooks, Thomas R. "Black Upsurge in the Unions." DISSENT 17 (March/April 1970): 124-34.

> Black union membership and activity within unions has increased in recent years. The expectation is that organized labor will become more involved in social movements and, as a result of the increased black participation, according to Brooks, reflect the early period of the Congress of Industrial Organizations. This view is contingent upon blacks not assuming middle-class values when they become active in the labor movement, which has been the case with ethnic groups using the labor movement for economic advancement.

Carter, Robert L., and Marcus, Maria L. "Trade Union Racial Practices and the Law. In THE NEGRO AND THE AMERICAN LABOR MOVEMENT, pp. 380-400. Edited by Julius Jacobson. Garden City, N.Y.: Doubleday & Co., 1968.

> Carter and Marcus find that union control of the grievance procedure and contract negotiations influences the condition of black workers. The National Labor Relations Board is the most influential regulator of these procedures. The authors review policies of the Board and recommend changes. The Board has prohibited unions from negotiating contracts which are detrimental to black workers, but only upon the filing of unfair labor practice charges by aggrieved workers.

Crowell, Erbin, Jr. "Equality and Organized Labor." CIVIL RIGHTS DIGEST 2 (Spring 1969): 33-36.

> Crowell examines the stated nondiscriminatory policies of organized labor. Despite breakthroughs, much remains to be done before official policy and actual practice are indistinguishable.

Derryck, Dennis A. "Minority Youth Can Be Apprentices." OCCUPATIONAL OUTLOOK QUARTERLY 11 (December 1967): 7-10.

> Derryck describes successful efforts to increase nonwhite participation in apprenticeship programs through preapprenticeship training. Cooperation of the building trade unions is of prime importance.

Dubinsky, Irwin. "Trade Union Discrimination in the Pittsburgh Construction Industry: How and Why it Operates." URBAN AFFAIRS QUARTERLY 6 (March 1971): 297-318. Tables.

> Dubinsky finds that de jure discrimination in the construction industry is difficult to prove. He recommends government promotion of black construction firms as a means for increasing black participation in the trades. But the primary vehicle is an increase in the supply of qualified black journeymen. Black contractors lack the financial capital to undertake more than small rehabilitation work. Government subsidized bonding of black contractors would improve their chances for increasing their market. The short supply of qualified black journeymen is a problem confronted by both white and black contractors who desire to increase black participation in the construction industry.

Gould, William B. "Black Workers in White Unions." NATION 209 (September 8, 1968): 203-6.

_____. "Discrimination and the Unions." DISSENT 14 (July/August 1967): 564-75.

Guinier, Edward. "Impact of Unionization on Blacks." In UNIONIZATION OF MUNICIPAL EMPLOYEES, pp. 173-81. Edited by Robert H. Connery. New York: Academy of Political Science, 1970.

> According to Guinier, blacks view unionization of public employees as both a potential benefit and liability. Unionization may increase the income of black workers but may also maintain the concentration of blacks in the lower positions of the occupational distribution. Union seniority rules may result in disproportionate numbers of blacks being released in the event of a reduction in the work force.

Hammerman, Herbert. "Minority Workers in Construction Referral Unions." MONTHLY LABOR REVIEW 95 (May 1972): 17-26. Tables.

> Hammerman finds that blacks and Spanish-Americans comprise relatively small proportions of the membership of contruction unions which refer workers to employers, particularly in the more skilled crafts. The proportions minorities comprise within the unions are

increasing, although at a very slow rate.

Hill, Herbert. "Black Protest and the Struggle for Union Democracy." ISSUES IN INDUSTRIAL SOCIETY 1 (1969): 19-29.

_____. "The Racial Practices of Organized Labor: The Contemporary Record." In THE NEGRO AND THE AMERICAN LABOR MOVEMENT, pp. 232-85. Edited by Julius Jacobson. Garden City, N.Y.: Doubleday & Co., 1969.

Hill observes that former affiliates of the Congress of Industrial Organizations are generally considered to be the most progressive in regard to blacks. This assumption is challenged by an examination of the International Ladies Garment Workers Union.

_____. "Racism and Organized Labor." NEW SCHOOL BULLETIN 28 (February 8, 1971).

Since the passage of the 1964 Civil Rights Act, discrimination by unions has become covert through testing procedures and educational requirements. The practice of deferring the admittance of blacks into craft unions until all white workers are employed is immoral and illegal, according to Hill, because discrimination has prevented their participation in the trades. Racial quotas should be utilized even during periods of unemployment.

Kovarsky, Irving. "Apprentice Training Programs and Racial Discrimination." IOWA LAW REVIEW 50 (Spring 1965): 755-76.

Kovarsky finds that a modification of the Taft-Hartley Act's prohibition of the closed shop by the Supreme Court, whereby unions and employers can negotiate exclusive hiring hall arrangements as long as unions agree to refer union and nonunion workers, has effectually given unions control over the labor supply. This control increases the difficulty blacks have in gaining entrance to the trades because of the restrictions placed on the total supply of labor and the inclination of the unions to show preference for friends and relatives of members.

_____. "Racial Barriers in Apprentice Training Programs." In HUMAN RESOURCES DEVELOPMENT, pp. 91-115. Edited by Edward B. Jakubauskas and C. Phillip Baumel. Ames: Iowa State University Press, 1967.

Kovarsky observes that among the reasons for low black participation in apprenticeship training programs are a failure of blacks to take advantage of existing opportunities because of distrust of white-dominated institutions, poor educational preparation, lack of information about apprenticeship opportunities, and inadequate financial resources to continue in apprenticeship programs during periods of high unemployment. It has been shown that black participation in apprenticeship programs of the various trades varies inversely with the lengths of indenture of the trades.

Leggett, John C. CLASS, RACE, AND LABOR. New York: Oxford University Press, 1968. 252 p. Tables.

. Leggett examines the degree of class consciousness among black and
white workers in Detroit, the determinants of class consciousness,
and implications for future public policy. He finds that among both
black and white union members, those who are recent migrants
from rural areas have the greatest degree of class consciousness.
As the rate of migration from rural areas to urban areas subsides,
the degree of class consciousness should also decline.

Lipset, Seymour. "Negroes and the Labor Movement." NEW POLITICS 1
(Spring 1962): 135–41).

Lipset examines the internal structure of organized labor. He finds
that national union leaders promote racial equality at least verbally,
while local unions are slow to increase their black membership and
encourage the participation of black members within the union.
The primary reason for the difference between local and national
unions is that local union activities are conducted more democrat-
ically than at the national level and, therefore, more likely to
reflect the prejudices of the union's membership.

McCauley, John S. "Increasing Apprenticeship Opportunities through Pre-Em-
ployment Training." In RESEARCH IN APPRENTICESHIP TRAINING, pp. 113-
20. The Center for Studies in Vocational and Technical Education, University
of Wisconsin, 1967.

Among the advantages of government-sponsored preemployment
training are that employers incur reduced training costs and are
more willing to hire minority group members who generally constitute a large proportion of the trainees. Whether a trainee gains
entrance to apprenticeship is directly correlated to the degree of
union and management participation. Where unions do not cooper-
ate in the formulation and operation of the "outreach" project,
successful placement of blacks has been minimal.

Marshall, F. Ray. "Black Workers and the Unions." DISSENT 19 (Winter
1972): 295–302.

There is likely to be very little resistance by whites to further ad-
vances by blacks on the job, except in the case of preferential treatment of unqualified blacks. Upgrading black workers so they are qualified would mitigate unfavorable reactions on the part of whites.

_____. THE NEGRO AND ORGANIZED LABOR. New York: John Wiley
& Sons, 1965. 327 p. Tables.

The development of the black's relationship with organized labor
is traced. Marshall describes the current racial practices of unions
and makes policy recommendations. The book essentially provides
an update of the type of survey Northrup conducted in 1944. By
1965, de jure discrimination became harder to identify due to state
antidiscrimination laws, except in the South which did not enact
fair employment practice laws.

. "The Position of Minorities in the American Labor Movement." In LABOR IN A CHANGING AMERICA, pp. 238-51. Edited by William Haber. New York: Basic Books, 1966.

Marshall finds that the complete elimination of racial discrimination in the labor movement would not equalize the black's position because of handicaps resulting from past discrimination. The labor movement's major concern should be with positive measures to improve the black's actual employment levels as well as his opportunities. This goal can be achieved by maintaining a high level of employment and improving the quality of education and training in the black community. Full employment would reduce the resistance of whites and give blacks greater incentive to train.

. "Union Racial Practices." In THE NEGRO AND EMPLOYMENT OPPORTUNITY, pp. 152-73. Edited by Herbert R. Northrup and Richard L. Rowan. Ann Arbor: University of Michigan Press, 1965.

Marshall finds that labor unions no longer bar blacks by formal means. Segregation by informal means is not restricted to the South. Craft unions appear to be the most exclusionary because of the control they wield over the supply of labor. Craft unions attempt to restrict their membership, while industrial unions attempt to organize all workers. It is debatable whether craft unions' restrictions on black workers are the result of racial discrimination or an effort to restrict the supply of labor and to allocate openings to friends and relatives.

Marshall, F. Ray, and Briggs, Vernon M., Jr. EQUAL APPRENTICESHIP OPPORTUNITIES: THE NATURE OF THE ISSUE AND THE NEW YORK EXPERIENCE. Ann Arbor: University of Michigan-Wayne State University Institute of Labor and Industrial Relations, 1968. 91 p. Tables.

Marshall and Briggs describe the apprenticeship training system, the obstacles to increased minority group participation, and the outreach program of the New York City Workers Defense League. The WDL outreach project is an effort by a private civil rights organization to recruit and train black youth to pass entrance examinations for admission into apprenticeship training programs. The program has been quite successful. However, the greatest increase in minority participation in any construction union occurred in 1962. At that time the International Brotherhood of Electrical Workers Local 3 actively sought to increase the minority participation and used subjective criteria, which were in existence prior to virtually all unions' conversion to the administration of entrance examinations.

. "Negro Participation in Apprenticeship Programs." In RESEARCH IN APPRENTICESHIP TRAINING, pp. 155-69. Madison: The Center for Studies in Vocational and Technical Education, University of Wisconsin, 1967.

Marshall and Briggs provide statistics on the extent of black participation in apprenticeship programs. A major factor accounting for low black participation rates is the educational inequality perpetuated by the public education system. Apprentice outreach projects which attempt to improve the reading, writing, and mathematical skills of black apprenticeship applicants have been successful at increasing the number of black apprentices.

_____. "Remedies for Discrimination in Apprenticeship Programs." INDUSTRIAL RELATIONS 6 (May 1967): 303-20.

Marshall and Briggs find that government sanctions have not been especially successful in gaining entrance for blacks into apprenticeship programs, though they may have had the effects of creating a climate which is conducive to change, motivating unions and employers to formalize apprenticeship standards and programs, and raising qualifications for apprenticeship. Programs which increase the supply of blacks qualified for apprenticeship have been more successful, such as apprenticeship outreach projects whereby blacks are recruited and trained to pass entrance examinations for apprenticeship.

_____. THE NEGRO AND APPRENTICESHIP. Baltimore, Md.: Johns Hopkins Press, 1967. 283 p. Tables.

Marshall and Briggs find that the reasons for the failure of blacks to gain entrance into apprenticeship programs for the skilled trades include employer and union resistance, and inadequate education, training, and labor market information for blacks relative to whites. Government-sponsored programs to increase minority participation have achieved success in those instances where employers and unions have cooperated, particularly in the area of preemployment training. The authors describe the conditions which led to the current policy of "home-town plans." Despite integration of previously segregated work forces and an increase in the total number of black apprentices, the rate of progress was slow. The major reasons are labor union insistence upon competitive written and oral examinations, which constituted a deviation from the previous policy of a subjective selection process which gave preference to friends and relatives. "Home-town plans," which established goals and timetables for representative minority participation, are a return to the subjective selection process.

Maurizi, Alex. "Minority Membership in Apprenticeship Programs in the Construction Trades." INDUSTRIAL AND LABOR RELATIONS REVIEW 25 (January 1972): 200-206.

Maurizi uses an investment model to show that a reason for low minority participation in the construction trades is that the increase in earnings after completion of training relative to income during the period of training is lower for minorities than for whites. Increasing the income incentive for serving an apprenticeship may be a more effective means for increasing minority participation than an antidiscrimination policy.

Michigan Civil Rights Commission. EMPLOYMENT DISTRIBUTION STUDY OF THE CONSTRUCTION INDUSTRY IN MICHIGAN. Lansing: Michigan

Civil Rights Commission, 1966.

The report provides an excellent analysis of the operation of the labor market in the construction industry and how it excludes minority group workers. Particular emphasis is placed upon the direct admission process whereby workers become journeymen without completing an apprenticeship. Placing emphasis upon increasing black participation in apprenticeship will delay the achievement of proportionate black representation in the building trade unions.

Northrup, Herbert R. ORGANIZED LABOR AND THE NEGRO. New York: Harper & Brothers, Publishers, 1944. 312 p. Tables.

Northrup examines the racial practices of organized labor during and prior to World War II. De jure discrimination was not very prevalent except in the railroad brotherhoods and the sheet metal workers union, at least in the sense of having specific provisions in their constitutions. Through less formal discriminatory practices, the majority of unions restricted the employment opportunities of blacks. Notable exceptions were the trowel trade unions and packinghouse workers.

O'Hanlon, Thomas. "The Case Against the Unions." In THE NEGRO AND THE CITY, pp. 104-21. Time-Life Books. New York: 1968.

O'Hanlon finds that the labor union practices which harm blacks include the hiring hall, seniority system, and apprenticeship. Strong governmental action would reduce the effectiveness of organized labor in maintaining control over who shall work and, in the case of craft unions, the number of workers.

Pati, Gopal C., and Waller, Dennis E. "Organized Labor and the Disadvantaged." PUBLIC PERSONNEL REVIEW 32 (April 1971): 66-70.

The seniority provisions in labor-union-negotiated contracts make recently hired black workers the first to be affected by a layoff. In unionized skilled trades, preference is often shown for friends and relatives of members. Governmental policies to increase black participation have often been unable to surmount union resistance.

Rapping, Leonard A. "Union-Induced Racial Entry Barriers." JOURNAL OF HUMAN RESOURCES 5 (Fall 1970): 447-74. Tables.

Rapping estimates the effect of collective bargaining on the proportion of nonwhites in major industries for major occupational groups. Time series data covering the period 1910-60 are also examined in which the rate of change in the proportion of nonwhites is related to the existence or growth of union activities. On the average, according to Rapping, collective bargaining heightens racial entry barriers. One might also view the effect of unions as raising wages relative to nonunion industries, thereby increasing the supply of labor available to unionized industries. Because of educational and labor market information differences

between blacks and whites, whites may be disproportionately represented in unionized industries.

"Reaching Out for Apprentices." MANPOWER 1 (June 1969): 8-13.

The article describes the joint efforts of unions, civil rights organizations and the federal government to increase minority participation in apprenticeship programs. These efforts include active recruitment of minorities at schools and community social organizations, the establishment of apprenticeship information centers at
state employment offices, and training programs designed to assist
minority applicants to pass examinations for apprenticeship jointly
administered by unions and employers. Craft union resistance is the
most formidable barrier to increased black participation in apprenticeship programs because of their predominant influence on joint
union-management apprenticeship committees.

Rosenberg, Bernard. "Torn Apart and Driven Together: A Portrait of a UAW
Local in Chicago." DISSENT 19 (Winter 1972): 61-69.

Black workers constitute a low proportion of skilled workers at an
automobile plant. Obstacles to increased participation are experience, education, supervisor recommendations, and the low wages
of apprenticeship. The practice of rating apprenticeship applicants
according to scores on competitive examinations occurred around
1964 largely as a result of black efforts to increase their participation in the skilled trades. Prior to that period, subjective entrance criteria were utilized. A return to more subjective entrance
criteria might enable more blacks to enter the trades.

Rowan, Richard L. "Discrimination and Apprentice Regulation in the Building
Trades." JOURNAL OF BUSINESS 40 (October 1967): 435-47. Tables.

Rowan examines the racial employment practices of four construction
unions in Philadelphia and finds them to be in violation of federal
government apprenticeship selection procedures. The major source
of difficulty in the so-called objective entrance procedures is the
oral examination. Applicants with friends or relatives in the trade
score consistently higher on the oral exam than black applicants.
Unions are remiss on providing adequate information on application
procedures to the black community.

Slaiman, Donald. "Equal Employment and the Unions." THE AMERICAN FED-
ERATIONIST 74 (December 1967): 14-17.

Slaiman relates the official position of organized labor toward
equal employment opportunity. As early as 1944, the American
Federation of Labor and Congress of Industrial Organizations both
supported fair employment practices legislation. Slaiman describes
the role of the Department of Civil Rights of the AFL-CIO in assisting the Equal Employment Opportunity Commission in cases of
discrimination.

Spero, Sterling D., and Harris, Abram L. THE BLACK WORKER--THE NEGRO AND THE LABOR MOVEMENT. New York: Columbia University Press, 1931. 509 p.

> Spero and Harris trace the employment condition of black workers from slavery through the 1920s and describe how blacks were excluded from the skilled trades after emancipation. They provide an historical perspective which may be useful in analyzing current problems of racial exclusion from unions comprised of skilled workers.

Strauss, George. "Apprenticeship: An Evaluation of the Need." In EMPLOYMENT POLICY AND THE LABOR MARKET, pp. 300-25. Edited by Arthur M. Ross. Berkeley: University of California Press, 1965.

> Strauss finds that the nation's need for skilled construction workers is being fulfilled, because the purpose of apprenticeship is to provide the most highly skilled members of the construction industry's labor force. The implication of this study for minorities is that gaining access to apprenticeship programs may not result in an appreciable number of jobs nor representative participation in the building trade unions. The primary reason is the vast majority of workers who gain entrance through the "back door": they acquire training in other industries or complete a portion of apprenticeship and gain entrance into the unions during periods of peak demand for construction workers, when union and employer skill requirements are less rigid.

Strauss, George, and Ingerman, Sidney. "Negro Discrimination in Apprenticeship." HASTINGS LAW JOURNAL 16 (February 1965): 285-331.

> Strauss and Ingerman observe that the obstacles confronting blacks in gaining entrance into apprenticeship programs entail more than merely the discriminatory practices of unions and employers. Job market information channels and minority education are additional obstacles. While racial prejudice cannot be discounted, building tradesmen have traditionally resisted all outside control of the collective bargaining relationship, maintaining that nepotism is both moral and proper. The craft unions probably exercise greater control than employers over the number and selection of apprentices, since friends and relatives constitute approximately 50 percent of all apprentices.

United States Department of Labor. NEGROES IN APPRENTICESHIP. Washington, D.C.: Manpower Administration, 1967. 38 p. Sold by Government Printing Office.

> The report identifies the obstacles to increased participation in apprenticeship programs by blacks as lack of available information and poor education. The report also discusses improved communication about opportunities in apprenticeship through the formation of Apprentice Information Centers.

Watters, Pat. "Workers, Black and White in Mississippi." DISSENT 19 (Winter 1972): 70-77.

> Watters describes efforts to promote cooperation among black and white trade unionists in Mississippi. Barriers to cooperation can be overcome by appeals to the commonality of working class interests.

Chapter 10

BLACKS AND GOVERNMENTAL
LAW AND POLICY

Chapter 10

BLACKS AND GOVERNMENTAL LAW AND POLICY

Albin, Peter S., and Stein, Bruno. "The Constrained Demand for Public Assistance." JOURNAL OF HUMAN RESOURCES 3 (Summer 1968): 300-311. Tables.

Albin and Stein examine the provisions of public assistance programs and find that eligibility requirements vary substantially between jurisdictions. Eligibility is also subject to administrative decisions, which can alter the number of recipients. The result, according to the authors, is that one cannot make valid comparisons between governmental jurisdictions.

America, Richard [F., Jr.]. "Antitrust and Race." BUSINESS AND SOCIETY REVIEW 2 (Summer 1972): 47.

America proposes the application of antitrust laws against white-dominated firms and the transfer of ownership to blacks. While this proposal might achieve an equalization of black-white incomes, it may result in an increase in national consumption expenditures and the price level. This and other political impracticalities make the proposal's adoption highly unlikely.

Baratz, Joan C. "Neo-Knownothingism: New Constraints on Research in the Black Community." URBAN AND SOCIAL CHANGE REVIEW 5 (Spring 1972): 75-79.

Bayley, David H., and Mendelsohn, Harold. MINORITIES AND THE POLICE. Glencoe, Ill.: Free Press of Glencoe, 1969. 209 p.

Bell, Duran, Jr. "Bonuses, Quotas, and the Employment of Black Workers." JOURNAL OF HUMAN RESOURCES 6 (Summer 1971): 309-20.

Bell compares the consequences for employers and black workers of racial quotas with training grant systems. The quota system is preferable to training grants on the grounds that the bonus tends to reward firms for having poor presubsidy ethnic ratios and provides the opportunity for profiteering on the part of racist employers, whereas the quota system benefits black workers without rewarding racism.

A modified subsidy system is devised which incorporates the advantages of both quota and bonus with few of the disadvantages of either.

Berger, Monroe. EQUALITY BY STATUTE. Garden City, N.Y.: Doubleday & Co., 1967. 253 p.

Berger traces the development of antidiscrimination laws. The impact of the laws has been less than originally anticipated due to the difficulty of proving de jure discrimination and the reluctance of aggrieved persons to file complaints. The agencies charged with enforcement of the laws are generally underfinanced and understaffed.

Berghe, Pierre L. van den. "The Benign Quota: Panacea or Pandora's Box." AMERICAN SOCIOLOGIST 6 (June 1971): 40-43.

According to Berghe, racial employment quotas perpetuate inequality by reinforcing racial distinctions within a society. This observation, however, rests on the assumption that there can in fact be a "melting pot" in the United States.

Bloomfield, Neil Jon. "Equality of Educational Opportunity: Judicial Supervision of Public Education." SOUTHERN CALIFORNIA LAW REVIEW 43: 275-306.

According to Bloomfield, periodic judicial review of the recommendations made in legal cases involving equality of education is necessary as new evidence on the effectiveness of various approaches to equal opportunity evolves. The question raised is whether the judiciary should adopt this role and go beyond the circumstances fostering a desegregation or equalization of expenditures case. It is questionable whether they have the power or the expertise.

Bogart, Leo, ed. SOCIAL RESEARCH AND THE DESEGREGATION OF THE U.S. ARMY. Chicago: Markham Publishing Co., 1969. 393 p.

Bogart finds that since the time of the integration of the U.S. Army in 1948, notable improvements have occurred in the morale of nonwhite troops. The degree of de facto segregation has declined, but the Army has not been sheltered from the racial strife existent in civilian society.

Bonfield, Arthur E. "The Substance of American Fair Employment Practices Legislation II--Employment Agencies, Labor Organizations, and Others." NORTHWESTERN UNIVERSITY LAW REVIEW 62 (March/April 1967): 19-44.

Boyce, Richard J. "Racial Discrimination and the National Labor Relations Act." NORTHWESTERN UNIVERSITY LAW REVIEW 65 (May/June 1970): 232-58.

Boyce reviews major National Labor Relations Board decisions in cases involving racial discrimination. The vast majority of cases have been filed against labor unions. In general, the Board has followed a course which closely parallels United States Supreme Court decisions and Federal Government statutes.

Brofenbrenner, Martin. "A Working Library on Riots and Hunger." JOURNAL OF HUMAN RESOURCES 4 (Summer 1969): 378-89.

Brofenbrenner critically reviews the "Report of the National Advisory Commission on Civil Disorders, Hunger U.S.A.," and "Hunger and Malnutrition in the United States."

Bryenton, Gary L. "Employment Discrimination: State FEP Laws and the Impact of Title VII of the Civil Rights Act of 1964." In DE FACTO SEGREGATION AND CIVIL RIGHTS. Edited by Oliver Schroeder, Jr., and David F. Smith. Buffalo, N.Y.: William S. Hein and Co., 1965.

Bryenton makes a comprehensive study of state and federal fair employment practice laws. One-half of the complaints filed are dismissed for lack of evidence. Of the other half pursued by the commissions, 95 percent are settled through conciliation without a public hearing and often do not result in the hiring or promotion of the complainant.

Bullock, Paul. EQUAL OPPORTUNITY IN EMPLOYMENT. Los Angeles: University of California Institute of Industrial Relations, 1966. 114 p.

Bullock traces the development of equal employment opportunity laws at the state and federal levels. He describes the investigative process under the law, and union and management efforts to combat discrimination. In general, the laws have failed to fulfill their anticipated impact.

Carson, Clarence B. THE WAR ON THE POOR. New Rochelle, N.Y.: Arlington House, 1969. 283 p.

In attempting to assist the poor, the government merely worsens their condition by inhibiting their incentive to work and reducing through higher taxes the amount of investment capital which would create jobs for the poor.

Carte, Gene E. "Police Representation and the Dilemma of Recruitment." ISSUES IN CRIMINOLOGY 6 (Winter 1971): 85-95.

Carte finds that increased demand from the minority community for more black policemen and increased wage competition with other economic sectors for black workers will aggravate the problem of making police departments more representative of the racial composition of urban areas. The solution may be to raise the wages of policemen and thereby attract qualified black applicants who might otherwise go to private industry.

Carter, Robert L. "Equal Educational Opportunity for Negroes--Abstraction or Reality." LAW FORUM (Summer 1968): 160-88.

Despite evidence that the quality of education is substantially poorer in all-black schools as compared to integrated schools, the Court's intention in Brown v. Board of Education was a prohibition of segregation, not a mandate for integration where de facto segregation exists. Carter concludes that the failure of the courts to mandate integration denies blacks equal educational opportunities.

Cassell, Frank H. "Equal Employment Opportunity: A Challenge to the Employment Service." EMPLOYER SERVICE REVIEW 3 (August 1966): 1-3. Tables.

The hiring and promotion process can be nondiscriminatory through a clear definition of job requirements, the evaluation of applicants, and the use of tests which relate only to job requirements. A major difficulty with this proposal, according to Cassell, is designing employee selection procedures which are directly job related and receive the affirmation of employee selection personnel.

Cloward, Richard A., and Piven, Frances F. "The Poor Against Themselves." NATION, November 25, 1968, pp. 558-62.

Cloward and Piven find that the welfare system erodes family structure and work incentive of the poor.

Cohen, Robert H. "Welfare: Race and Reform." CIVIL RIGHTS DIGEST 2 (Fall 1969): 20-25.

Cohen finds that the higher the proportion of nonwhites comprising public assistance programs in the various states, the lower the average monthly allotment. The reasons for this phenomenon are not entirely clear. They may include discrimination, but states with low welfare payments also have low per capita incomes.

Cohen, Wilbur J. "Government Policy and the Poor: Past, Present, and Future." JOURNAL OF SOCIAL ISSUES 26 (1970): 1-9.

A federal welfare system administered through the social security program and the creation of public service jobs would alleviate many deficiencies of the present welfare system. Cohen cites the inequality of welfare benefits among the states and the lack of employment opportunities among the poor.

Coleman, Francis F. "Title VII of the Civil Rights Act: Four Years of Procedural Elucidation." DUQUESNE LAW REVIEW 8 (Winter 1969-70): 1-31.

Coleman reviews judicial interpretations of the equal employment opportunity provisions of the 1964 Civil Rights Act. In general, the scope of the law has been broadened by the judiciary.

Colfax, J. David. "Pressure toward Distortion and Involvement in Studying a

Civil Rights Organization." HUMAN ORGANIZATION 25 (Summer 1966): 140-49.

> Colfax discusses and illustrates the difficulties for researchers to maintain scientific objectivity while studying civil rights organizations. The result is that governmental policy is often dictated by white middle-class values and is contrary to the values of minority groups.

Congressional Quarterly Service. REVOLUTION IN CIVIL RIGHTS. Washington, D.C.: Congressional Quarterly Service, 1965. 94 p.

> The report traces the development of the civil rights movement, equal opportunity legislation, and judicial decisions from the end of World War II until the passage of the Civil Rights Act of 1964.

Cooksey, Frank C. "The Role of Law in Equal Employment Opportunity." BOSTON COLLEGE INDUSTRIAL AND COMMERCIAL LAW REVIEW 7 (Spring 1966): 417-30.

> The law has a limited capacity to deal with equal opportunity employment. Its role will expand in the future, according to Cooksey, particularly with the advent of negotiations between government and employers concerning programs designed to increase minority employment.

Cousens, Frances Reissman. PUBLIC CIVIL RIGHTS AGENCIES AND FAIR EMPLOYMENT: PROMISE VS. PERFORMANCE. New York: Frederick A. Praeger, Publishers, 1969. 163 p.

> Employment discrimination has not been substantially reduced since the enactment of fair employment laws. Among the problems encountered are the difficulty of proving de jure discrimination, inadequate financing and staffing of agencies charged with enforcement of the law, and the failure of agencies to negotiate enforceable affirmative action plans.

Fletcher, Arthur A., and Wilks, John L. ESTABLISHMENT OF RANGES FOR THE IMPLEMENTATION OF THE REVISED PHILADELPHIA PLAN FOR COMPLIANCE WITH EQUAL EMPLOYMENT OPPORTUNITY REQUIREMENTS OF EXECUTIVE ORDER 11246 FOR FEDERALLY-INVOLVED CONSTRUCTION. Washington, D.C.: U.S. Department of Labor, 1969. 20 p.

> Fletcher and Wilks analyze annual vacancy rates in selected building trade unions in the Philadelphia area and demonstrate how increased numbers of blacks could be admitted without altering total labor supply. The report is an attempt to answer a major objection to affirmative action plans for increasing black participation in the construction industry.

Forslund, Morris A. "Standardization of Negro Crime Rates for Negro-White Differences in Age and Status." ROCKY MOUNTAIN SOCIAL SCIENCE JOURNAL 7 (April 1970): 151-60.

> Forslund observes that a substantial portion of the difference in

black-white crime rates can be explained by the relatively younger
age and higher concentration of blacks in low-paying jobs. By
holding age and economic status constant, Forslund observes no
appreciable difference in black-white crime rates.

Fusfeld, Daniel R. "Training for Minority Groups: Problems of Racial Imbalance
and Segregation." In NEGROES AND JOBS, pp. 338-54. Edited by Louis A.
Ferman et al. Ann Arbor: University of Michigan Press, 1968. Tables.

The exclusion of blacks from manpower training programs financed
by the federal government and segregation within existing programs
is substantial, particularly in the South, despite federal policy to
the contrary. An important reason is the administration of manpower programs at the local level by state agencies. In spite of
these shortcomings, manpower programs have had a significant impact in upgrading skills, providing new training opportunities, and
opening new areas of employment for black workers.

Galbraith, John K., et al. "Toward Greater Minority Employment." CURRENT,
no. 133 (October 1971), pp. 22-29.

The authors assert that employment policy has been almost entirely
concerned with low-paying, entry level jobs. They propose a federal law establishing quotas for minority groups in higher salary
jobs. According to their plan, training programs would be established so that the quotas could be met.

Garfinkel, Herbert, and Cahn, Michael D. "Racial-Religious Designations,
Preferential Hiring, and Fair Employment Practices Commissions." LABOR LAW
JOURNAL 20 (June 1969): 357-72.

Garfinkel and Cahn find that lower educational attainment is ac-
countable for about one-third of the white-nonwhite income differential, while the remaining two-thirds is attributable to discrimination by employers. Racial designations on employment records
should be kept in order to identify and resolve cases of discrimination. The authors also conclude that quota employment is not
an equitable solution to the problem.

Gibbs, Inez L. "Institutional Racism in Social Welfare." CHILD WELFARE
50 (December 1971): 582-87.

Gibbs documents instances where public funds were earmarked for
minority people and this purpose was not fulfilled. The reason is
that public welfare agencies either utilized the funds to assist
whites or in a manner which deteriorated the position of minorities.

Glazer, Nathan. "Beyond Income Maintenance--A Note on Welfare in New
York City." PUBLIC INTEREST, no. 16 (Summer 1969), pp. 102-20.

Glazer examines the effects of a guaranteed annual income plan
on poverty level incomes, the incentive to work, and family

structure. He doubts that income maintenance will improve the work incentive, but if income levels could be lifted out of the level of poverty, which debilitates the health of the poor, the stability of poor families should improve. The present welfare system has assured only subsistence living conditions, increased the dissolution of family structures, and hampered the work incentive by penalizing male-headed households and those who take low-paying jobs.

Gould, William B. "The Emerging Law Against Racial Discrimination." NORTHWESTERN UNIVERSITY LAW REVIEW 64 (July/August 1969): 359-86.

According to Gould, the law has not been effectively utilized in remedying the results of past discrimination in cases involving nepotism and segregated seniority lists. Nepotism is not only reflected in discriminatory hiring practices (de jure discrimination) but also restricts job market information channels (de facto discrimination). Segregated seniority lists, informally negotiated in the past, restrict the movement of blacks into higher-paying occupational categories and increase the degree of layoffs among black workers when declines in economic activity occur.

_____. "Racial Discrimination, the Courts, and Construction." INDUSTRIAL RELATIONS 11 (October 1972): 380-406.

Antidiscrimination litigation in the construction industry is really being tried for the first time. Court-imposed quotas offer the prospect of equality. Gould reviews recent court decisions.

Hare, Nathan. "A Study of the Black Fighter." BLACK SCHOLAR 3 (November 1971): 2-9.

Hare finds that black fighters come from low socioeconomic backgrounds and remain in that class upon retirement from the ring. A major reason for this impoverished condition upon retirement is that the boxing game is regulated by the individual states, and nothing has been done to improve the retirement condition of boxers.

Harrison, Bennett. "National Manpower Policy and Public Service Employment." NEW GENERATION 53 (Winter 1971): 3-14.

Harrison finds that completion of high school has a substantially smaller return for nonwhites than for whites. He recommends greater emphasis on policies to increase the demand for labor, including greater employment in the public sector in deference to government policies to increase the educational attainment of blacks.

Herbert, Stanley P., and Reischel, Charles L. "Title VII and the Multiple Approaches to Eliminating Employment Discrimination." NEW YORK UNIVERSITY LAW REVIEW 4 (May 1971): 449-85.

The 1964 Civil Rights Act has provided the federal government with
two major avenues for combating employment discrimination. The
Equal Employment Opportunity Commission receives complaints from
aggrieved parties and attempts to adjudicate the cases. In addition,
the Commission investigates employers and unions in order to discern
patterns of discrimination, and attempts to negotiate affirmative action plans whereby the employer and/or union establishes a time-
table for achieving acceptable goals of minority representation.

Hill, C. Russell. "Two Income Maintenance Plans, Work Incentives, and the
Closure of the Poverty Gap." INDUSTRIAL AND LABOR RELATIONS REVIEW
25 (July 1972): 545-55.

A principal objective of income maintenance schemes is to preserve
incentive to work while reducing the poverty gap. Hill investigates
two types of income maintenance plans--a wage subsidy and a vari-
ant of the negative income tax. He suggests that a wage subsidy
is as effective as the negative income tax in raising family income
and, thereby, closing the poverty gap, while, at the same time,
the wage subsidy preserves a relatively large degree of work incentive among the working poor.

Hill, Herbert. "The New Judicial Perception of Employment Discrimination:
Litigation Under Title VII of the Civil Rights Act of 1964." UNIVERSITY OF
COLORADO LAW REVIEW 43 (March 1972): 243-68.

Hill reviews the legal precedents established under the 1964 Civil
Rights Act. Further sanctions, such as voiding licenses to do business, are necessary to counteract institutionalized patterns of employment discrimination. The political feasibility of this proposal
is remote.

. "Twenty Years of State Fair Employment Practice Commissions: A
Critical Analysis with Recommendations." BUFFALO LAW REVIEW 14 (Fall
1964): 22-64.

Hill recommends widespread fundamental change in the operation of
state fair employment practice commissions. Among the deficiencies
of the commissions are that they only investigate discrimination when
complaints are filed, and they fail to compel employers to develop
positive programs to increase minority participation.

Hoos, Ida R. RETRAINING THE WORK FORCE. Berkeley: University of
California Press, 1967. 281 p.

Hoos examines government sponsored training programs in the San
Francisco area.

Hunter, Kenneth W. "Jurisdictional Conflicts in Minority Employment Relations:
NLRB and EEOC." UNIVERSITY OF SAN FRANCISCO LAW REVIEW 2 (October 1967): 149-63.

Hunter examines the issue of dual jurisdictions by the National
Labor Relations Board and the Equal Employment Opportunity Commission over employment discrimination cases.

Ingram, Timothy H. "Fair Employment: The Machinery Continues to Rust."
WASHINGTON MONTHLY 4 (December 1972): 37-45.

Ingram chronicles the failure of the federal government to cancel
contracts with private corporations which restrict the employment
of minorities, and to negotiate enforceable affirmative action plans
with the employers.

Jackson, Raymond. "Job Discrimination and the Use of Bonuses." AMERICAN
JOURNAL OF ECONOMICS AND SOCIOLOGY 32 (October 1973): 351-66.
Tables.

Jackson describes a bonus scheme combining both a penalty for
discrimination and an incentive for attaining the objective of increased employment opportunities for blacks. The burden of find-
ing procedures and methods by which additional blacks can be
attracted and qualify for employment is placed on the employer
rather than the government. This is more efficient because the
expertise in determining the essential skills and requirements for
successful job performance lies with firms, not government commissions.

Javitz, Jacob K. "A Marshall Plan for Americans." SOCIAL SERVICE OUT-
LOOK 1 (October 1966): 1-2.

Javitz recommends substantial increases in government spending on
public assistance, education, and housing.

Jenkins, Timothy Lionel. "Study of Federal Effort to End Job Bias: A History,
a Status Report, and a Prognosis." HOWARD LAW JOURNAL 14 (Summer 1968):
259-329.

Jenkins traces the development of the federal equal employment
policy, notes its deficiencies, and advocates greater initiative by
the government, such as quota employment and requiring employers
to institute training programs for blacks.

Kaplan, John. "Equal Justice in an Unequal World: Equality for the Negro--
The Problem of Special Treatment." NORTHWESTERN UNIVERSITY LAW RE-
VIEW 61 (July/August 1966): 363-410.

The major objection to racial quotas in employment is that lower-
socioeconomic class whites, who in many respects are in the same
class as blacks, would suffer. However, it is often middle and
upper-class whites who voice the loudest objections in specific
cases which appear to involve special treatment for blacks.

Kirkbridge, Joe B. "Familiar Faces Bridge Policy-Ghetto Gap." MANPOWER 1 (April 1969): 22-27.

Kirkbridge describes efforts to train minorities to be policemen in Oakland, California.

Klos, Joseph J. "Public Assistance, Family Allowances, or the Negative Income Tax?" NEBRASKA JOURNAL OF ECONOMICS AND BUSINESS 8 (Spring 1969): 16-31.

Klos compares existing public assistance programs with family allowance and negative income tax proposals. He recommends a modified negative income tax plan which provides social services to the poor. Klos's conclusion that the provision for social services is an economically beneficial program remains unproven.

Konvitz, Milton R., and Leskes, Theodore. A CENTURY OF CIVIL RIGHTS WITH A STUDY OF STATE LAWS AGAINST DISCRIMINATION. New York: Columbia University Press, 1961. 293 p. Tables.

Konvitz and Leskes provide an excellent analysis of antidiscrimination activities prior to the 1964 Civil Rights Act, which signified active federal involvement.

Krislov, Samuel. THE NEGRO IN FEDERAL EMPLOYMENT. Minneapolis: University of Minnesota Press, 1967. 157 p. Tables.

Krislov traces the development of the policy toward black employment in the federal government and analyzes the equal employment policies and performance of various federal agencies. In general, black employment is concentrated in lower echelon jobs with no agency achieving notable success in integrating higher-paying, higher-status jobs.

Landes, William M. "The Economics of Fair Employment Laws." JOURNAL OF POLITICAL ECONOMY 76 (July/August 1968): 507-52.

Relative wages, in 1959, were higher by about 5 percent and discrimination lower by 11 and 15 percent in states with fair employment laws as compared with states without these laws. Although such relative wage differences were not present in the states during 1949, the relative occupational distribution of nonwhite to white males remains unaffected by the passage of the laws.

Lekachman, Robert. "Can 'More Money' End Poverty?" DISSENT 14 (September/October 1967): 557-63.

Lekachman examines various proposals to eliminate poverty, and notes deficiencies in all proposals because of an inability to devise plans which simultaneously provide work incentives and eliminate poverty.

Leuthold, Jane H. "An Empirical Study of Formula Income Transfers and the Work Decision of the Poor." JOURNAL OF HUMAN RESOURCES 3 (Summer 1968): 312-23.

> Leuthold uses cross-section data to estimate the work disincentive from income transfers. In general, more work should be forthcoming except for a limited number of recipients.

Lockard, Duane. TOWARD EQUAL OPPORTUNITY: A STUDY OF STATE AND LOCAL ANTIDISCRIMINATION LAWS. New York: Macmillan Co., 1968. 150 p. Tables.

Lipsky, Michael, and Olson, David J. "Riot Commission Politics." TRANS-ACTION 6 (July/August 1969): 8-21.

> In the opinion of Lipsky and Olson, riot commission reports contain vague generalities and protect vested interests. The reports' conclusions are generally unacceptable to those empowered to effect change.

McVeigh, Edward J. "Equal Job Opportunity within the Federal Government." EMPLOYMENT SERVICE REVIEW 5 (July/August 1968): 42-47.

> McVeigh describes efforts of the federal government to increase minority employment within its own ranks.

Mann, Seymour Z. CHICAGO'S WAR ON POVERTY. Chicago: Center for Research in Urban Government, Loyola University, 1966. 62 p. Tables.

> Mann describes and analyzes the strengths and weaknesses of the agency charged with improving the condition of Chicago's poor. He also offers recommendations for procedural change.

Mayhew, Leon H. LAW AND EQUAL OPPORTUNITY: A STUDY OF THE MASSACHUSETTS COMMISSION AGAINST DISCRIMINATION. Cambridge, Mass.: Harvard University Press, 1968. 313 p.

Means, John E. "Fair Employment Practices Legislation and Enforcement in the United States." INTERNATIONAL LABOUR REVIEW 93 (March 1966): 211-47.

> Means traces the historical development of governmental efforts in the United States to promote equal employment opportunities. He emphasizes the degree of effectiveness of the various laws and generally finds them to be deficient. Among the problems are inadequate financing and staffing, difficulty of proving de jure discrimination, reluctance of aggrieved parties to file charges, and the failure of commissions to negotiate affirmative action plans.

Mencher, Samuel. POOR LAW TO POVERTY PROGRAM: ECONOMIC SECURITY POLICY IN BRITAIN AND THE UNITED STATES. Pittsburgh: University of Pittsburgh Press, 1967. 476 p.

Mencher traces and compares the development of governmental antipoverty policies in the United States and Great Britain.

Mindlin, Albert. "The Designation of Race or Color on Forms." PUBLIC ADMINISTRATION REVIEW 26 (June 1966): 110-18.

In an effort to eliminate a means for discrimination, employers have removed racial designations from application forms and personnel records. As a result, research is hampered and racial composition, as evidence of discrimination, is difficult to identify. Mindlin recommends reinstatement, with safeguards, of racial designations on employment records.

Moskos, Charles C., Jr. "The American Dilemma in Uniform: Race in the Armed Forces." ANNALS OF THE AMERICAN ACADEMY OF POLITICAL AND SOCIAL SCIENCES 406 (March 1973): 94-106. Tables.

Moskos provides statistics on black participation in the various branches of the Armed Forces over much of this century.

. "Minority Groups in Military Organization." In HANDBOOK OF MILITARY INSTITUTIONS, pp. 271-89. Edited by Roger W. Little. Beverly Hills, Calif.: Sage Publications, 1971.

Moskos finds that the attitude of blacks toward military service is generally more favorable than that of whites. This may be a reflection of the military's ability to maintain greater equality; and, according to Moskos, black reenlistment is facilitated by the authoritarian nature of the military.

Murray, Paul. "The Negro Woman's Stake in the Equal Rights Amendment." HARVARD CIVIL RIGHTS-CIVIL LIBERTIES LAW·REVIEW 6 (March 1971): 253-59.

Murray examines the relative economic disadvantage of nonwhite males and females and finds females receive only 65 percent of the income of males while experiencing one-third more unemployment. The double impediment of racial and sexual discrimination makes the constitutional protection of the Equal Rights Amendment imperative. Murray advocates the passage of the amendment.

National Advisory Commission on Civil Disorders. REPORT OF THE NATIONAL ADVISORY COMMISSION ON CIVIL DISORDERS. Washington, D.C.: U.S. Government Printing Office, 1968. 425 p. Tables.

The "Kerner Report" examines the causes of the ghetto riots of the 1960s and recommends a vast restructuring of American society, because the primary cause of racial strife is "white racism" in the economic and social spheres.

Norgren, Paul H., and Hill, Samuel E. TOWARD FAIR EMPLOYMENT. New York: Columbia University Press, 1964. 296 p.

Norgren and Hill analyze fair employment practice laws and the
commissions which administer these laws. They conclude that fair
employment laws are the most effective approach to combating
racial discrimination in employment, but that certain substantive
and procedural matters should be changed.

Nowell, Reynolds S. "A Plan for Youth Employment." In THE DISADVAN-
TAGED POOR: EDUCATION AND EMPLOYMENT, pp. 323-43. By Task Force
on Economic Growth and Opportunity. Washington, D.C.: Chamber of Commerce of the United States, 1966.

Nowell finds that an increase in the minimum wage reduces the
employment opportunities of disadvantaged youth. The author
presents alternative proposals among which are the repeal of minimum wage laws, training of the disadvantaged, and subsidies to
employers who hire marginal workers.

Olson, Robert H., Jr. "Employment Discrimination Litigation: New Priorities
in the Struggle for Black Equality." HARVARD CIVIL RIGHTS-CIVIL LIBERTIES
LAW REVIEW 6 (December 1970): 20-60.

Orcutt, Guy H., and Orcutt, Alice G. "Incentive and Disincentive Experimen-
tation for Income Maintenance Policy Purposes." AMERICAN ECONOMICS
REVIEW 58 (September 1968): 754-72.

The Orcutts describe the variables and methods for studying the
incentives and disincentives of income maintenance programs.
The major problem appears to be the cost of conducting experi-
mentation in order to verify incentive and disincentive effects.

Payne, Ethel. "The Blacks Pay the Price of Postal Efficiency." CITY 5
(Winter 1971): 10-13.

Automation and the location of facilities in the suburbs are two
factors eroding the employment position of blacks in the postal
service. Because blacks comprise a large percentage of low seniority employees in the Postal Service, reductions in manpower
affect them adversely.

"The Philadelphia Plan and Strict Racial Quotas on Federal Contracts." UCLA
LAW REVIEW 17 (March 1970): 817-36.

The REVIEW examines the prospects for the legality of racial employment quotas under the 1964 Civil Rights Law. Arguments sup-
porting and denying the legality appear equally strong, and it will
be up to the courts to decide. The prospect of the Supreme Court
failing to rule upon the issue and perpetuating the current limbo
condition is not foreseen.

Powers, Thompson, ed. EQUAL EMPLOYMENT OPPORTUNITY: COMPLIANCE AND AFFIRMATIVE ACTION. New York: National Association of Manufacturers, 1969. 125 p.

Powers discusses the roles of the Equal Employment Opportunity Commission, Office of Federal Contract Compliance, Justice Department, other federal agencies, state fair employment practice commissions, and local equal employment agencies. He answers questions posed by businessmen during a conference regarding the function, powers, and limitations of the agencies.

Purdy, John W. "Title VII: Relationship and Effect on State Action." BOSTON COLLEGE INDUSTRIAL AND COMMERCIAL LAW REVIEW 7 (Spring 1966): 525-33.

Purdy examines the effectiveness of the 1964 Civil Rights Act's provision that complainants first file with state fair employment practice commissions and concludes that the procedure is inefficient. He recommends that complainants have initial access to the Equal Employment Opportunity Commission.

Rachlin, Carl. "Title VII: Limitations and Qualifications." BOSTON COLLEGE INDUSTRIAL AND COMMERCIAL LAW REVIEW 7 (Spring 1966): 473-94.

The 1964 Civil Rights Act would be more effective if small employers presently excluded from its jurisdiction were included. Exclusion of blacks is apparent in small, white-owned businesses operating in the ghetto. Extention of the law to cover these small businesses, according to Rachlin, would increase black employment opportunities.

Rainwater, Lee. "Open Letter on White Justice and the Riots." TRANSACTION 4 (September 1967): 22-32.

Rainwater finds that the major reason for black discontent is economic inequality. The short run solution is income transfer programs. In the long run, adequate job training, enforcement of antidiscrimination laws, and the maintenance of high aggregate demand are necessary.

Reeves, Earl J. "Making Equality of Employment Opportunity a Reality in the Federal Service." PUBLIC ADMINISTRATION REVIEW 30 (January/February 1970): 43-49.

According to Reeves, affirmative action versus the passive policy of nondiscrimination enforcement is now the policy in federal employment, because education and job market information deficiencies made the latter policy ineffective. Affirmative policies include preemployment job training and efforts to reduce cultural bias on examinations. The degree to which this change in policy has been effective is difficult to assess due to the relatively short time since the policy changed.

Rogers, Elijah B. "A Career in Municipal Government for Blacks–Why Not?" PUBLIC MANAGEMENT 54 (April 1972): 14-15.

> According to Rogers, the black domination of many large central cities and the election of black politicians have increased opportunities for employment in municipal government. Where these jobs represent a nontraditional form of employment, special recruitment and training efforts are viewed as a necessary precondition to an increase in minority representation.

Rohrlich, George F. "Guaranteed Minimum-Income Proposals and the Unfinished Business of Social Security." SOCIAL SERVICE REVIEW 41 (June 1966): 166-78.

> Rohrlich critiques various guaranteed income proposals. He recommends modification of the means test utilized under the present welfare system and expansion of manpower training and relocation programs.

————. "Work and Income Policies for the Negro in Urban Slums." In THE SOCIAL WELFARE FORUM, pp. 78-93. New York: Columbia University Press, 1968.

> Rohrlich recommends that the federal government establish new social service oriented occupations to be filled by unemployed blacks.

Rosen, Sumner M. "Manpower Issues for the Cities." URBAN AFFAIRS QUARTERLY 6 (September 1970): 22-32. Tables.

> Rosen finds a number of important deficiencies in manpower programs designed to upgrade urban blacks: virtually exclusive concentration on finding jobs for the young to the exclusion of older workers, accepting without question the qualifications established by employers, failure to adapt formal education to the needs of the potential unemployed, failure to provide incomes to the hard-core unemployed, and failure to improve labor market information channels.

Rosenbloom, David H. "Equal Employment Opportunity: Another Strategy." PERSONNEL ADMINISTRATION AND PUBLIC PERSONNEL REVIEW 1 (July/August 1972): 38-41.

> Rosenbloom finds that blacks are underrepresented in managerial positions with the federal government. This condition is largely due to an inability of blacks to place high on entrance examinations. He proposes that all who pass exams be eligible and that the order of employment be randomly assigned to individuals. Job performance would not be adversely affected.

Ross, David F. "Public Employment and the New Segregation in the South." GROWTH AND CHANGE 2 (January 1971): 29-33.

Ross observes that statistics on the degree of black employment in state and local governments are not adequate. From available data he observes that blacks are represented in token numbers within skilled labor, white-collar, and supervisory positions.

Rowan, Richard L., and Brudno, Robert J. "Fair Employment in Building: Imposed and Hometown Plans." INDUSTRIAL RELATIONS 11 (October 1972): 394-406. Tables.

In order to increase black participation in the building trades, the federal government imposed "home town plans" in some cities. In others, it provided the stimulus for the voluntary adoption of plans. Goals and timetables for achieving representative minority representation are stipulated in the plans. The authors describe two plans, but both have fallen short of expectations primarily because of a lack of government supervision.

Santos, Everett J. "New Weapon Against Job Discrimination." CIVIL RIGHTS DIGEST 2 (Summer 1969): 35-38.

Santos describes the function of the National Labor Relations Board in combating employment discrimination. Unfair labor practice charges can be brought against employers and unions which resort to racist appeals prior to NLRB elections. In the determination of appropriate election units, the NLRB can include minority workers who might otherwise be excluded from the bargaining unit.

Schneiderman, Leonard. "Racism and Revenue Sharing." SOCIAL WORK 17 (May 1972): 44-49.

The difference in welfare benefits between states cannot be explained solely by differences in per capita income. Low per capita income states have the highest proportions of nonwhite recipients. Revenue sharing would give state governments even more power over the welfare system and increase the possibility of racial discrimination.

Sheilds, Robert, and Thompson, Lee. "A Guaranteed Annual Income: The Case for...The Case Against...." THE CONFERENCE BOARD RECORD 5 (September 1968): 30-33.

Shields and Thompson summarize the major arguments for and against the guaranteed annual income proposal.

Sovern, Michael S. LEGAL RESTRAINTS ON RACIAL DISCRIMINATION IN EMPLOYMENT. New York: Twentieth Century Fund, 1966. 270 p.

Sovern outlines the major provisions of state and federal fair employment laws and the agencies which administer these laws. He concludes that the process has largely been ineffective due to deficiencies both in the laws and in their administrators. Sovern recommends granting greater investigatory powers to the agencies and increasing the operating budgets of the agencies.

Sutton, David. "The Military Mission Against Off-Base Discrimination." In PUBLIC OPINION AND THE MILITARY ESTABLISHMENT, pp. 149-79. Edited by Charles C. Moskos, Jr. Beverly Hills, Calif.: Sage Publications, 1971.

Sutton describes Defense Department efforts to reduce off-base discrimination against minority servicemen. In education, segregation has been reduced dramatically due to the threat by the federal government to withhold subsidies. Housing segregation remains a problem.

"Their Goal: To Become 'Men in Blue'." INDUSTRIAL BULLETIN 45 (July 1966): 2-4.

Efforts to increase the number of minority group members in the New York City Police Department include active recruiting and training designed to equip minorities to pass the civil service examination.

Tobias, Henry, and Woodhouse, Charles. ETHNIC MINORITIES IN POLITICS. Albuquerque: University of New Mexico Press, 1968. 131 p.

Tobias and Woodhouse make an extensive study of minority influence on the electoral process. In general, minorities have not participated in proportion to their potential composition of the electorate. They conclude that in recent years their participation has increased due to greater awareness of the impact of political decisions upon their lives and liberalization of voting requirements.

Tobin, James. "On Improving the Economic Status of the Negro." In NEGROES AND JOBS, pp. 530-50. Edited by Louis A. Ferman et al. Ann Arbor: University of Michigan Press, 1968.

Full employment and high economic growth rates are necessary conditions for any specific program attacking black poverty and are the most powerful factors determining the economic status of blacks. Expansionary government macro-economic policies appear to be more powerful instruments for achieving black-white income equality than micro-oriented manpower policies.

_____. "Raising the Incomes of the Poor." In AGENDA FOR THE NATION, pp. 77-116. Edited by Kermit Gordon. Washington, D.C.: Brookings Institution, 1968. Tables.

Tobin analyzes alternatives to the present welfare system such as income tax credits, children's allowances, and the negative income tax. He favors the negative income tax as the most economically efficient system within the constraint of being the most likely sanctioned by the political system.

Turner, John B. "Education for Practice with Minorities." SOCIAL WORK 17 (May 1972): 112-18.

Turner outlines procedures for attracting minority people into the
social work field and improving the education of social workers
dealing with minorities.

United States Commission on Civil Rights. RACISM IN AMERICA AND HOW
TO COMBAT IT. Washington, D.C.: Clearinghouse Publication, Urban Series
No. 1. 43 p. Sold by Government Printing Office.

The Commission finds that racism occurs in housing, education, and
employment and yields economic, political, and psychological benefits to whites. To combat racism the behavior of whites must change
and the capabilities of nonwhites must improve. Government-sponsored training and housing programs will accomplish the latter, if
conducted on a large scale. According to the report, positive contacts between blacks and whites will accomplish the former in time.

United States Congress. GUARANTEED MINIMUM INCOME PROGRAMS USED
BY GOVERNMENTS OF SELECTED COUNTRIES. Washington, D.C.: U.S.
Government Printing Office, 1968. 87 p.

This Congressional report outlines major provisions of guaranteed
annual income plans utilized in other countries.

United States Department of Labor. BREAKTHROUGH FOR DISADVANTAGED
YOUTH. Washington, D.C.: U.S. Department of Labor, Manpower Administration, 1969. 256 p.

The report evaluates fifty-five government-sponsored experimental
projects designed to improve the employability of disadvantaged
youth.

_____. LEGAL DEPARTMENT DETAILS CONTRACTORS' EQUAL JOB OPPOR-
TUNITY STANDARDS. Washington, D.C.: U.S. Department of Labor, Office
of Information, 1972. 23 p.

The Department of Labor report indicates that federal contractors
must determine the extent of minority employment at their firms
and develop affirmative action plans for increasing minority participation. This marks a departure from the traditional governmental
policy of processing complaints of discriminatory policy, to one of
challenging de facto segregation in the labor market.

Warren, Roland L. POLITICS AND THE GHETTOS. New York: Atherton
Publishers, 1969. 214 p.

Warren examines the government policies which perpetuate the existence of the ghetto, such as low-cost housing projects, urban
renewal, and the welfare system. Black input into the political
system is minimal, and, as might be expected, the outcome is
equally marginal.

Weaver, Robert C. NEGRO LABOR--A NATIONAL PROBLEM. New York:

Harcourt, Brace, and Co., 1946.   329 p.

> Weaver examines the occupational status of black workers and makes
> policy recommendations remarkably similar to those presently under
> consideration.   He provides a good historical perspective on New
> Deal quota employment policies.

Wickenden, Elizabeth.   "Sharing Prosperity: Income Policy Options in Affluent
Society."   In TOWARDS FREEDOM FROM WANT, pp. 3-33.   Edited by Sar
A. Levitan et al.   Madison: Industrial Relations Research Association Series,
1968.

> Wickenden investigates various strategies for improving the income
> of the poor, including changing the attitudes of the nonpoor, in-
> creasing the political and market power of the poor, and changing
> the economic institutional structure.

Wolfbein, Seymour L.   EDUCATION AND TRAINING FOR FULL EMPLOYMENT.
New York: Columbia University Press, 1967.   264 p.

> Wolfbein describes the scope and ideological basis of manpower
> training efforts in the United States.   Concentration upon manpower
> policies as a means for improving the employment condition of
> minorities is most consistent with the ideology of a free enterprise
> system.

Chapter 11

AMERICAN INDIANS

Chapter 11

AMERICAN INDIANS

Bennett, Robert L. A REPORT. Washington, D.C.: Bureau of Indian Affairs, U.S. Department of the Interior, 1966. 9 p. Sold by Government Printing Office.

> Bennett summarily describes the role of the United States Bureau of Indian Affairs in influencing the educational, residential, and economic condition of Indians. The report suggests means for improving the relationship between the government agency and Indians.

Bigart, Robert J. "Indian Culture and Industrialization." AMERICAN ANTHROPOLOGIST 74 (October 1972): 1180-88.

> Bigart contends that the factory system is incompatible with Indian culture. He recommends a restructuring of production techniques so as to be compatible with the communal system of work organization which is a part of Indian culture.

Brophy, William A., and Aberle, Sophie D. THE INDIAN: AMERICA'S FINISHED BUSINESS. Norman: University of Oklahoma Press, 1967. 236 p. Tables.

> This volume is a report of the Commission on the Rights, Liberties, and Responsibilities of the American Indian. The authors trace the development of the Indians' legal status. The Indians' economic condition is difficult to assess because of a lack of quantifiable data. Among the problems described are inadequate employment opportunities in reservation areas, fragmented land holdings, and insufficient capital to improve land. Industrial development is minimal, but some notable successes have occurred where manpower training and capital are available. The structure and function of the Bureau of Indian Affairs is described. The book provides the best overall description of the socioeconomic conditions of American Indians, their legal status, and the obstacles to improvement.

Burnette, Robert. THE TORTURED AMERICANS. Englewood Cliffs, N.J.: Prentice-Hall, 1971. 176 p.

Burnette analyzes the legal status of American Indians and their socioeconomic conditions. He recommends a vast restructuring of the relationship between the federal government and the Indians. The book is probably most valuable for its vivid and proven examples of the Indians' plight.

Cahn, Edgar S., ed. OUR BROTHER'S KEEPER: THE INDIAN IN WHITE AMERICA. New York: New Community Press, 1969. 206 p.

The articles in this volume describe the relationship between the United States Bureau of Indian Affairs and the Indians, and vividly portray their socioeconomic condition. The major point of the volume is that federal government policy has been inconsistent toward Indians and altered through the years in order to attain the best, white advantages of land ceded to the Indians.

Castro, Tony. "Crisis of the Urban Indian." HUMAN NEEDS 1 (August 1972): 29-30.

Castro describes the impoverished condition of American Indians residing in cities and the failure of social service agencies to improve that condition. The high alcoholism and suicide rates are compounded by cultural dislocation. White-dominated social service agencies cannot relate to the cultural dislocation.

Christiansen, John R. SOCIAL AND ECONOMIC CHARACTERISTICS OF THE UTE INDIANS ON THE UNITAFOURAY RESERVATION: 1965. Provo, Utah: Institute of American Indian Studies and Research, Brigham Young University, Social Science Research Bulletin no. 4, 1966. 20 p. Tables.

Statistical descriptions of American Indian tribes are notably sparse. Christiansen's profile of the socioeconomic characteristics of the Ute is suggestive of the type of data necessary to conduct more meaningful economic research.

Cohen, Warren H., and Mause, Philip J. "The Indian: The Forgotten American." HARVARD LAW REVIEW 81 (June 1968): 1818-58.

Cohen and Mause provide a comprehensive summary of the position of American Indians under the law. The divestment of Indian lands by the government and the failure of the government to abide by the spirit of treaties which it signed with the Indians are among the darkest chapters in American history. If these conditions were absent today, the degree of injustice would still be irreparable. But these practices continue through the policies of the United States Bureau of Indian Affairs.

Collier, Peter. "The Red Man's Burden." RAMPARTS 8 (February 1970): 26-38.

Collier criticizes the United States Bureau of Indian Affairs for attempting to undermine Indian culture and for exploiting Indian land. He provides some interesting examples to substantiate his allegations. Collier makes a case for transfer of control over reservations to the Indians.

Dennis, Lloyd B. "American Indians: Neglected Minority." EDITORIAL RESEARCH REPORTS 11 (August 24, 1966): 621-40.

Upon reviewing the socioeconomic condition of American Indians, Dennis concludes that among American minority groups Indians are at the very bottom in terms of employment, income, education, and housing. He advises the government to grant greater control to Indians over government-financed programs operated on reservations and to improve the quality of natural resources on the reservations in order to foster economic independence.

Gaillard, Frye. "We'll Do it Our Own Way for Awhile." RACE RELATIONS REPORTER 3 (January 3, 1972): 21-27.

Gaillard describes efforts by American Indians to govern the educational system by operating their own schools. The failure of white-dominated educational institutions to respond to the needs of Indian culture is the prime reason for this development.

Hansen, Niles M. "The Indians." In URBAN AND REGIONAL DIMENSIONS OF MANPOWER POLICY, pp. 229-75. Washington, D.C.: U.S. Department of Labor, 1970.

Hansen provides a socioeconomic profile of American Indians. He advocates expansion of both assistance in securing employment off the reservation and the location of industry on the reservation. The economic condition of the Indian has been affected more by movement away from the reservation than by the location of industry on the reservation.

Hertzberg, Hazel W. THE SEARCH FOR AN AMERICAN INDIAN IDENTITY. Syracuse, N.Y.: Syracuse University Press, 1971. 362 p.

Hertzberg contends that American Indians are caught in an identity crisis between the maintenance of traditional culture and adaptation to modern industrialized society. The dilemma is compounded by the shifting emphasis of government policy between assimilation and separation.

"Indians Weave a New Image." MANPOWER 2 (April 1970): 9-13.

The article describes an Indian-owned and -operated carpet firm and government-sponsored training programs utilized by the firm. The coordination of manpower training programs with the development of business enterprises capable of employing the newly trained workers continues to be the exceptional case on reservations.

Joint Economic Committee, United States Congress. AMERICAN INDIANS:

FACTS AND FUTURE--TOWARD ECONOMIC DEVELOPMENT FOR NATIVE AMERICAN COMMUNITIES. New York: Arno Press, 1970. 566 p. Tables.

The volume contains studies by various authors summarizing current economic conditions among American Indians. Serious deficiencies in current statistical information make adequate evaluation of federal policies difficult. The study makes recommendations for economic development, job training, and industrialization efforts on the part of the government. Rectifying the land title problem is viewed as necessary for agricultural development. The report is inconsistent because it recommends highly structured capitalistic programs for government-controlled economic development although it asserts that Indians do not desire complete assimilation into capitalistic society. This inconsistency might be alleviated by granting the Indians complete discretionary control over government funds. Apart from this objection, the volume stands as the best treatise on American Indian economic development.

Josephy, Alvin M., Jr. RED POWER: THE AMERICAN INDIANS' FIGHT FOR FREEDOM. New York: American Heritage Press, 1971. 259 p.

The civil rights revolution by America's minority groups now includes the Indians. Josephy describes the efforts of Indian organizations to develop a self-identity for their people and to challenge federal government and white-dominated private organizations whose policies are viewed as detrimental to the best interests of the Indian people.

Levitan, Sar A., and Hetrick, Barbara. BIG BROTHER'S INDIAN PROGRAMS --WITH RESERVATIONS. New York: McGraw-Hill Book Co., 1971. 228 p.

Sar and Hetrick examine the obstacles to economic development of Indian reservations. These include lack of capital investment, geographical isolation, and inadequate government programs. They propose comprehensive government planning on the order equal to that required for an underdeveloped country including both agricultural reform and industrial development.

Levy, Jerrold E. "The Older American Indian." In OLDER RURAL AMERICANS, pp. 221-38. Edited by Grant E. Youmans. Lexington: University of Kentucky Press, 1967.

Levy states that the erosion of traditional tribal customs has imposed especially severe burdens upon elderly American Indians. While the tribe traditionally accorded authoritarian status to the elderly and provided economic security, "acculturation" has altered their status.

McFarland, J. T. "The Constitutional Rights of the American Indian." VIRGINIA LAW REVIEW 51 (1965): 121-42.

The Constitution and subsequent laws of the United States grant American Indians a special status applicable to no other group of citizens. Indians are subject to tribal laws, the councils which administer those laws, and state and federal laws and courts. A myriad of rules determining jurisdictions has evolved over the years.

Parmee, Edward A. FORMAL EDUCATION AND CULTURE CHANGE: A MODERN APACHE INDIAN COMMUNITY AND GOVERNMENT EDUCATION PROGRAMS. Tucson: University of Arizona Press, 1968. 132 p.

Education programs sponsored by the federal government are deficient in providing the tools necessary for American Indians to adapt to an industrial society. Among the reasons for the failure of education are a lack of parental involvement in school programs, an impoverished home life for most students, and a misunderstanding of Indian culture by school administrators.

Scott, Loren C. "The Economic Effectiveness of On-The-Job Training: The Experience of the Bureau of Indian Affairs in Oklahoma." INDUSTRIAL AND LABOR RELATIONS REVIEW 23 (January 1970): 220.

Scott conducts a cost-benefit analysis of an on-the-job training program for American Indians. The study indicates that trainees benefited by an average annual increase in earnings of nearly $2,000, secured at no private cost to themselves. Social costs of the training were about $1,000 but social benefits were about $2,000. Estimated social benefit-cost ratios for the program range from 7.6 to 29.4, depending upon the discount rate and the time period used in the calculation.

Seldman, Neil N. "The American Indian: April 1966." INDUSTRIAL AND LABOR RELATIONS FORUM 5 (January 1969): 395-437.

Seldman provides a descriptive analysis of the social, educational, and economic condition of American Indians. He recommends treatment by the government on the order necessary to transform an underdeveloped economy into an industrialized society.

Sorkin, Alan [L.] "Poverty and Dropouts--The Case of the American Indian." GROWTH AND CHANGE 1 (July 1970): 14-18. Tables.

Sorkin observes that the school dropout rate for American Indians is significantly dependent upon family income and adult educational attainment upon the reservation. A major reason why the school dropout rate among reservation Indians is much higher than for non-Indians is that the income differential for Indian high school graduates over dropouts is very small, a fact which reflects the depressed economic conditions upon reservations. Data for nonreservation Indians is sparse. An interesting study would be the income differential between nonreservation graduates and dropouts educated both on and off reservations.

_____. AMERICAN INDIANS AND FEDERAL AID. Washington: Brookings Institution, 1971. 192 p. Tables.

Sorkin examines the socioeconomic condition of Indians, government policies which perpetuate that condition, and proposes a comprehensive policy of economic development to be conducted by the government. Economic development policy must be concerned with fostering new industry as well as agricultural reform. Emphasis upon industrial development to the exclusion of agricultural development belies the cultural heritage of the Indians and neglects the economic field of endeavor in which their greatest comparative advantage exists. Among the most pressing issues for agricultural development is the consolidation of fragmented land holdings.

_____. "American Indians Industrialize to Combat Poverty." MONTHLY LABOR REVIEW 29 (March 1969): 19-25.

Sorkin describes two types of methods for establishing industry on American Indian reservations. The first process is for white-owned businesses to locate on reservations in order to take advantage of the surplus labor available. The second is for Indians to launch their own business enterprises. In both cases, manpower development and training is a necessary precondition. In the second case, training is an even more vital aspect due to the paucity of managerial skills.

Steiner, Stan. THE NEW INDIANS. New York: Harper & Row, Publishers, 1968. 348 p.

Steiner describes a growing awareness among American Indians that their cultural heritage must be preserved. Indians also realize that the major reason for their plight is the dependent relationship they bear to the federal government.

Striner, Herbert E. "Toward a Fundamental Program for the Training, Employment and Economic Equality of the American Indian." In FEDERAL PROGRAMS FOR THE DEVELOPMENT OF HUMAN RESOURCES, Subcommittee of Economic Progress of the Joint Economic Committee. Washington, D.C.: Congress of the United States, 1968. Sold by Government Printing Office.

Striner examines the socioeconomic condition of American Indians. Based upon that analysis, he recommends a vast increase in federal government efforts to improve the basic education and occupational training of the Indians. In order to utilize the improved labor supply, the development of economic enterprises on reservations is advised.

Stucki, Larry R. "The Case Against Population Control: The Probable Creation of the First American Indian State." HUMAN ORGANIZATION 30 (Winter 1971): 393-99.

Stucki predicts that due to the declining white population and increasing Navaho population in the area, a real potential exists for the creation of an Indian state in portions of Arizona, New Mexico,

and Utah. The probability of the federal government allowing the
formation of such a state appears unlikely. As an argument against
population control, the author seems to be pressing for a pipe dream.
In fact, the realization of his dream might even worsen the condition of the Indians, given the sparse natural resources of the area
and its miniscule tax base.

United States Bureau of Indian Affairs. AMERICAN INDIANS AND THE FED-
ERAL GOVERNMENT. Washington, D.C.: U.S. Department of the Interior,
1965. 26 p. Tables.

The report provides an excellent summary of the legal relationship
between the federal government and American Indians, and describes
various programs conducted by the government. Missing, however,
is an assessment of their actual impact.

United States Department of Health, Education, and Welfare. INDIAN POV-
ERTY AND INDIAN HEALTH. Washington, D.C.: March 1964. Tables.
Sold by Government Printing Office.

Unfortunately, this the most up-to-date, comprehensive analysis of
income and health data available to the researcher. Based upon
a special study, it provides a vivid portrayal of the impoverished
condition under which American Indians live.

United States Department of the Interior. STATISTICS CONCERNING INDIAN
EDUCATION. Washington, D.C.: Annual Report. Tables. Sold by Government Printing Office.

This annual statistical report on American Indian education is valuable to the researcher interested in conducting time series analyses.
The reports would be more meaningful if data were provided on a
microlevel.

Urvant, Ellen. "From Sea to Shining Sea." VISTA VOLUNTEER 5 (May 1969):
24-31.

Urvant assesses the condition of Passamaquoddy Indians in Maine.
Poverty and unemployment are the rule. Government policy attempts to lure them off the land, conflicting with the Indians'
traditional tie to the land. Urvant describes an effort to bring
industry to the reservation.

Weaver, Thomas. INDIANS IN RURAL AND RESERVATION AREAS. Sacramento:
State of California Advisory Commission on Indian Affairs, 1966. 129 p. Tables.

Weaver describes the socioeconomic condition of American Indians
in California: incomes are low; unemployment rates are high; educational attainment lags behind that of the population as a whole.
In summary, Indians, whether they reside on reservations or off,
resemble subsistence farmers in underdeveloped nations.

Welch, W. Bruce. "The American Indian (A Stifled Minority)." JOURNAL OF NEGRO EDUCATION 38 (Summer 1969): 242-46.

> Welch outlines the historical oppression of American Indians. He criticizes efforts to establish colleges on reservations as an attempt to rekindle a futile hope that the Indian nations will again exist. This integrationist view disregards the desire on the part of some Indians for self-determination and independence from federal government education programs, which they view as the cause of the Indians' poor self-concept.

Wilson, Roderick C. "Papago Indian Population Movement: An Index of Culture Change." ROCKY MOUNTAIN SOCIAL SCIENCE JOURNAL 6 (April 1969): 23-32.

> Wilson chronicles the movement of Papago Indians from the reservation to the cities, the cultural shock they confront, and the apparent trend of movement back to the old culture. The issue of whether the Indians' condition is better off the reservation than on is unsettled as well as unsettling.

Chapter 12

SPANISH-AMERICANS

Chapter 12

SPANISH-AMERICANS

Aragon, Manuel. "Their Heritage--Poverty." AGENDA 2 (July 1966): 9-13.

Aragon vividly portrays the impoverished conditions under which many Mexican-Americans live. Poverty is intergenerational and is sustained by the deficiencies of educational and health care institutions.

Arias, Ronald. "The Barrio." AGENDA 2 (July 1966): 15-20.

Arias describes the housing, education, and other socioeconomic conditions of Mexican-Americans. He stresses improved education as a remedy to the socioeconomic deficiencies encountered. The primary value of this article is its descriptive summary.

Barrera, Mario, et al. "The Barrio as an Internal Colony." In PEOPLE AND POLITICS IN URBAN SOCIETY, pp. 465-98. Edited by Harlan Hahn. Beverly Hills, Calif.: Sage Publications, 1972.

The authors observe that it is inappropriate to compare Mexican-Americans with European migrants of an earlier period. The cultural assimilation and mobility through an education model of the latter is not an accurate prescription for people who are ethnically more identifiable. Treating the Chicano community as an internal colony is more appropriate.

"Bridge to the Barrios." MANPOWER 1 (December 1969): 10-14.

The article describes a federal government sponsored project (Service, Employment and Redevelopment) designed to improve the employability of Mexican-Americans. A possible research topic is an assessment of this program, which is not provided by this article nor indicated by a review of the literature.

Briggs, Vernon M., Jr. CHICANOS AND RURAL POVERTY. Baltimore: Johns Hopkins Press, 1973. 81 p. Tables.

According to Briggs, Chicanos residing in the rural Southwest are unable to achieve wealth and power because of the large-scale farming and ranching in the region and their lack of capital'. The flow of Mexican nationals across the border increases the labor supply and lowers wages. Briggs enumerates deficiencies in social insurance and manpower training programs.

Bullock, Paul. "Employment Problems of Mexican-Americans." INDUSTRIAL RELATIONS 3 (May 1964): 37-50. Tables.

Bullock examines the barriers to improved economic standing for Mexican-Americans. The prevalance of segregated housing and education and employer discrimination are the most important factors. Economic analysis of Mexican-Americans is hampered by a lack of data reflecting the group's "emergence."

Carter, Thomas P. MEXICAN-AMERICANS IN SCHOOL: A HISTORY OF EDUCATIONAL NEGLECT. Princeton, N.J.: College Entrance Examination Board, 1970. 235 p.

Mexican-Americans suffer from low educational attainment in terms of both years of education completed and quality of education received. Among the reasons for the perpetuation of this educational neglect is the failure of the schools to effectively regard the language and culture of Chicanos.

Casavantes, Edward. "Pride and Prejudice: A Mexican American Dilemma." CIVIL RIGHTS DIGEST 3 (Winter 1970): 22-27.

According to Casavantes, poverty, rather than inherent ethnic traits, accounts for the employment and educational problems of Mexican-Americans. Full development of potential is impeded by discrimination and false stereotypes. Recommendations are of a general nature and shed little light on concrete policy reforms.

Choldin, Harvey M., and Trout, Grafton D. MEXICAN AMERICANS IN TRANSITION. East Lansing: Michigan State University, 1971. 33 p. Tables.

Choldin and Trout describe the socioeconomic condition of Mexican-Americans in the State of Michigan, where Mexican-Americans constitute a small proportion of the total population. Their incomes are substantially lower than those of the general population. This condition appears to disprove the thesis that the reason for Mexican-American poverty in the Southwest is their high proportion of total population and their inability to assimilate, thereby making them targets for discrimination.

Clapp, Raymond F. "Spanish-Americans of the Southwest. In POVERTY IN AMERICA; BOOK OF READINGS, pp. 198-215. Edited by Louis A. Ferman et al. Rev. ed. Ann Arbor: University of Michigan Press, 1968. Tables and charts.

Clapp provides an excellent statistical profile of Spanish-Americans in terms of education distribution, unemployment, household composition, age distribution, labor market participation rates, occupational distribution, annual income, country of origin, and urban-rural residence. This is an excellent reference for locating sources of information on Spanish-Americans.

Clark, Margaret. HEALTH IN THE MEXICAN-AMERICAN CULTURE. Berkeley: University of California Press, 1970. 253 p.

Infant mortality and tuberculosis are more pronounced among Mexican-Americans than the general population. Lower life expectancies are attributable to a variety of factors including inadequate health care delivery systems and impoverished living conditions, particularly in migratory agricultural worker camps.

Cohen, Howard. "Statement before the Special Committee on Aging." HEARINGS ON AVAILABILITY AND USEFULNESS OF FEDERAL PROGRAMS AND SERVICES TO ELDERLY MEXICAN-AMERICANS, pp. 499-523. Washington, D.C.: U.S. Senate, Ninety-First Congress, November 20-21, 1969. Sold by Government Printing Office.

Cohen provides a chronicle of United States Department of Health, Education, and Welfare programs which affect the condition of elderly Mexican-Americans. While data on expenditures are provided, it is difficult to judge the impact of these programs on the basis of this evidence.

Felice, Lawrence G. "Mexican American Self-Concept and Educational Achievement." SOCIAL SCIENCE QUARTERLY 53 (March 1973): 716-37.

According to Felice, the influence of segregation on the educational attainment of Mexican-American students supports the integration policy of the schools. As with other racial and ethnic minorities, Mexican-American children have a poor self-concept in terms of their ability to achieve. This self-fulfilling prophecy is manifested at school.

Florez, John. "Chicanos and Coalitions as a Force for Social Change." SOCIAL CASEWORK 52 (May 1971): 269-73.

Florez states that non-Chicano-controlled institutions are deficient as forces for change in the socioeconomic condition of Mexican-Americans. He recommends the establishment and continued growth of existing Chicano-controlled community organizations.

Fogel, Walter [A.] "Job Gains of Mexican-American Men." MONTHLY LABOR REVIEW 91 (October 1968): 22-27. Tables.

The movement of Mexican-Americans out of agriculture has lagged behind that of the general population. The reasons for this lower rate of occupational transformation include differences in occupational preferences and occupational qualifications between Anglos and Chicanos. Discrimination is another factor.

_____. MEXICAN-AMERICANS IN SOUTHWEST LABOR MARKETS. Los Angeles: University of California at Los Angeles, Graduate School of Business Administration, 1967. 222 p. Tables.

> Fogel provides a comprehensive statistical description of Mexican-American workers in the region of the country where they are concentrated. Although correlation coefficients are not calculated, low incomes and high unemployment rates appear to be the result of low levels of educational attainment and discrimination. Residential concentration in areas with low rates of economic growth is also a factor.

Forbes, Jack D. "Race and Color in Mexican-American Problems." JOURNAL OF HUMAN RELATIONS 16 (First Quarter, 1968): 55-68.

> Forbes contends that Mexican-Americans are mostly of Indian blood, and that their impoverished conditions are largely the result of racial discrimination based upon visually identifiable race and color. This argument strengthens the view that research applicable to blacks and Indian Americans is relevant to problems of inequality encountered by Chicanos.

Galarza, Ernesto. "La Mula No Nacio Arisca." CENTER DIARY 14 (September/October 1966): 26-32.

> Galarza contends that mechanization has reduced the need for Mexican-American agricultural workers. He advises that Chicano farm workers adapt to other occupations. He concedes that this adaptation is difficult in view of educational and occupational training deficiencies.

Galarza, Ernesto, et al. MEXICAN-AMERICANS IN THE SOUTHWEST. Santa Barbara, Calif.: McNally and Loftin, 1969. 90 p.

> According to the authors, Mexican-Americans are employed in occupations characterized by capital substitution and are poorly educated. Elimination of poverty will only occur through community organizations which strive to eradicate discrimination by securing entrance into occupations where capital substitution is less eminent, and by improving the quality of education provided to Mexican-Americans.

Garcia, Alejandro. "The Chicano and Social Work." SOCIAL CASEWORK 52 (May 1971): 274-78.

> Garcia states that the social work profession perpetuates the economic and social inferiority of Mexican-Americans by not understanding their language and culture. Beyond the maintenance of impoverishment, social workers may cause psychological instabilities by the creation of roles which clients are expected to emulate.

Gonzalez, Nancie. THE SPANISH AMERICANS OF NEW MEXICO: A DIS-

TINCTIVE HERITAGE. Los Angeles: Graduate School of Business Administration, University of California, 1967. 149 p.

> Gonzalez provides a descriptive profile of Spanish-Americans in New Mexico. Spanish government land grants at the time of the Conquestedors established large estates and a feudal societal structure. Despite American statehood and progression into the 20th century, aspects of this heritage have survived.

Guerra, Manuel H. "Educating Chicano Children and Youth." PHI DELTA KAPPAN 53 (January 1972): 313-14.

> According to Guerra, Mexican-American children are treated as inferiors by the Anglo-dominated school system. Policy alternatives include reform of educational institutions to be more responsive to the needs of Chicano students and to be Chicano-dominated.

Hansen, Niles M. "Improving Economic Opportunity for the Mexican Americans." ECONOMIC AND BUSINESS BULLETIN 22 (Fall 1969): 1-14. Tables.

> According to Hansen, Mexican-Americans are not hampered by discrimination to the same degree as blacks. Disadvantage in the job market stems from lack of education and training, and Mexican nationals depress wages for citizens of Mexican-American extraction by increasing the supply of labor beyond what it would be if the federal government enforced immigration laws.

_____. "The Mexican Americans." In URBAN AND REGIONAL DIMENSIONS OF MANPOWER POLICY, pp. 276-319. Washington, D.C.: U.S. Department of Labor, 1970.

> Hansen provides a socioeconomic profile of Mexican-Americans. He attributes the poor economic condition to lack of employment skills, discrimination, low educational attainment, and residence in economically depressed areas. He recommends relocation in areas of increasing economic growth. Voluntary or government-sponsored relocation are both difficult to conceive.

Heller, Celia S. MEXICAN AMERICAN YOUTH: FORGOTTEN YOUTH AT THE CROSSROADS. New York: Random House, 1966. 113 p.

> Whether their parents are employed as migratory agricultural workers or they reside on farms or in the city, Mexican-American youth lead impoverished lives in terms of health care and educational attainment. Unresponsive health care delivery and school systems are major factors.

Linde, Jed, ed. OPERATION BUSINESS BREAKTHROUGH: A STUDY OF THE MANPOWER IMPLICATIONS OF SMALL BUSINESS FINANCING IN OAKLAND CALIFORNIA. Oakland, Calif.: Oakland Small Business Development Center, 1967. 160 p. Tables.

Among the major problems confronting Mexican-American entrepreneurs are inadequate capital formation potential and reliance upon customers whose low incomes impede profitability and business expansion. The expansion of credit availability and markets into white middle-class residential areas would greatly assist Chicano enterprises which are primarily of a retail nature.

Meier, Matt S., and Rivera, Feliciano. THE CHICANOS: A HISTORY OF MEXICAN AMERICANS. New York: Hill and Wang, 1972. 302 p.

Meier and Rivera trace the development of Mexican-American culture in the United States from the time of the native Indian population's submission to the Spanish Conquestedors. The book provides an excellent description of the factors accounting for the impoverished condition of Chicanos today.

Miller, Herman P. "Puerto Ricans, Mexicans, and Other Minorities." In RICH MAN, POOR MAN, pp. 87-104. New York: Crowell Publishing, 1971.

Miller observes that the educational attainment of Puerto Ricans in New York City is below that of any other ethnic minority and is an important reason for their economic disadvantage. He hypothesizes that Puerto Ricans in New York City are perhaps not any better situated economically than they would be in their native land, because they constitute the sector of the population in both New York City and Puerto Rico with the least economic potential.

Mittelbach, Frank G. "Understanding of Mexican-Americans." JOURNAL OF HOUSING 6 (June 1969): 296-98.

Mittelbach provides a synopsis of the socioeconomic condition of Mexican-Americans and their housing preferences, which may be of value to urban planners. Planners must develop housing programs within the context of Mexican-American culture by enlisting their cooperation and support.

Payne, William. "Mexican American Farmers: Victims of Neglect." CIVIL RIGHTS DIGEST 2 (Spring 1969): 37-38.

Payne describes the impoverished conditions under which Mexican-American farmers and their families exist. Small land holdings and tenant status are major causes of this subsistence condition which resembles the condition of farmers in underdeveloped countries.

Poston, Dudley L., and Alvirez, David. "On the Cost of Being a Mexican American Worker." SOCIAL SCIENCE QUARTERLY 53 (March 1973): 697-715.

Poston and Alvirez calculate wate differentials between Anglos and Mexican-Americans in various regions of the country. Differentials vary between regions. On the average, the wage differential is $900 for comparable educational and occupational groupings. A difficulty with the study is that while years of education are accounted for, achievement is not.

Ramirez, Henry M. "America's Spanish-Speaking: A Profile." MANPOWER 4 (September 1972): 31-34.

Ramirez gives the relative proportions that Cubans, Mexican-Americans, and Puerto Ricans comprise of the Spanish-speaking people in the United States, the geographical regions in chich they are concentrated, and statistics on their socioeconomic condition. The primary value of this article is that the researcher is provided with sources of informational data on Spanish-Americans.

Rogler, Lloyd H. MIGRANT IN THE CITY: THE LIFE OF A PUERTO RICAN ACTION GROUP. New York: Basic Books, 1972. 251 p.

As recent migrants to the city, Puerto Ricans are confronted with the cultural difficulties faced by other migrant groups in earlier years. These problems are compounded by the changing nature of the labor market and the declining demand for unskilled labor. Within this framework, Rogler describes the efforts of a community organization to improve conditions.

Samora, Julian, and Lamanna, Richard A. MEXICAN-AMERICANS IN A MIDWEST METROPOLIS: A STUDY OF EAST CHICAGO. Los Angeles: Graduate School of Business Administration, University of California, 1971. 164 p.

Samora and Lamanna describe the socioeconomic condition of Mexican-Americans in East Chicago, Illinois. The assimilation process and an improvement of economic status appear to be retarded primarily by low educational attainment. Low educational attainment is a result of the unresponsiveness of the educational system toward Spanish speaking students.

Schmidt, Fred H. "Job Caste in the Southwest." INDUSTRIAL RELATIONS 9 (October 1969): 100-110. Tables.

Schmidt observes that it is unlikely that Mexican-Americans in the Southwest attained 8.2 percent of all crafts jobs--which represent close to the 9.3 percent of the region's labor force--and would be qualified for only 5 percent of clerical and sales positions. Clerical and sales positions require greater public contact but less skill than crafts jobs. According to Schmidt, a "job caste" appears to exist within the region.

_____. SPANISH SURNAMED AMERICAN EMPLOYMENT IN THE SOUTHWEST. Washington, D.C.: U.S. Equal Employment Opportunity Commission, 1970.

247 p. Tables. Sold by Government Printing Office.

Schmidt provides statistics on the occupational distribution, income, and employment regularity of Spanish-surnamed workers in the Southwest. He criticizes federal government's immigration policies which create increased labor market competition for Spanish-American citizens by allowing illegal aliens to continue working in the Southwest.

Servin, Manuel P. THE MEXICAN-AMERICANS: AN AWAKENING MINORITY. Beverly Hills, Calif.: Glencoe Press, 1970. 235 p. Tables.

Servin observes that while Mexican-Americans are not the most oppressed minority, they are the most ignored by scholars. This study contains classic contemporary articles which attempt to trace and analyze the life and society of Mexican-Americans. Servin exposes myths about innate lack of ambition, innate violence, and other sterotypes.

Shaw, Ray. "Overlooked Minority." WALL STREET JOURNAL 167 (May 3, 1966).

Written during turbulent years of the black civil rights struggle, Shaw examines the socioeconomic condition of Mexican-Americans and concludes that public concern and government policy has disregarded Chicanos. The primary value of this article is that it provides researchers with a point of departure when examining later efforts on the part of Chicanos to improve their condition.

Skrabanek, R. L. "Language Maintenance among Mexican Americans." CIVIL RIGHTS DIGEST 4 (Spring 1971): 18-24.

Skrabanek observes that, to a large degree, Mexican-Americans retain their use of the Spanish language at home. This fact has implications which are often ignored in the planning and implementation processes of education and manpower programs.

Taylor, Ronald B. SWEATSHOPS IN THE SUN: CHILD LABOR ON THE FARM. Boston: Beacon Press, 1973. 216 p.

Taylor vividly describes the condition of Mexican-American agricultural workers with particular emphasis upon their children who work in the fields instead of attending school. Educational attainment is retarded by the complicity of public officials, inadequate health care, and poor dietary and sanitary conditions.

Turner, Paul R. "Academic Performance of Mexican Americans." INTEGRATED EDUCATION (May/June 1973): 3-6.

Turner observes that Mexican-American children from small families and whose fathers are employed achieve at higher levels in school than children from large families and whose fathers are unemployed. Turner concludes that socioeconomic class is a determinant of educational achievement.

United States Bureau of the Census. "Persons of Spanish Origin in the United States: November 1969." CURRENT POPULATION REPORTS, Series P-20, no. 213. Washington, D.C.: February 1971. 39 p. Tables. Sold by Government Printing Office.

> This special census report provides statistics on the education, income, labor force participation rate, and degree of employment regularity of Spanish-Americans. This survey is a prerequisite for research on Spanish-Americans.

United States Commission on Civil Rights. THE MEXICAN AMERICAN. Washington, D.C.: U.S. Government Printing Office, 1967. 69 p. Tables.

> This special report of the Commission describes the socioeconomic condition of Mexican-Americans, their frustrations in attaining an improvement in that condition, and the institutional arrangements which perpetuate inequality. Conditions are appreciably worse for migrant farm workers and their families than any other group in the Chicano community.

. MEXICAN AMERICANS AND THE ADMINISTRATION OF JUSTICE IN THE SOUTHWEST. Washington, D.C.: U.S. Government Printing Office, 1970. 135 p.

> Police misconduct, bias in the jury system, and inadequate representation in agencies which administer justice warrant the mistrust of Mexican-Americans toward the criminal justice system.

Vazquez, Hector S. "Puerto Rican Americans." JOURNAL OF NEGRO EDUCATION 38 (Summer 1969): 247-56.

> Vazquez describes the relationship between the public schools and the Puerto Rican community. By eliminating the cultural bias of the white-dominated educational system, the number of years of schooling completed and educational achievement should improve.

Williams, J. Allen, et al. SOCIAL SCIENCE QUARTERLY 53 (March 1973): 710-15.

> The authors attribute the differential income between Anglos and Mexican-Americans to both lower educational attainment and lower-socioeconomic class family background. A problem with this study is its failure to account for income differentials attributable to discrimination. As in many other studies, discrimination is taken as a residual value.

INDEXES

AUTHOR INDEX

In addition to authors, this index includes all editors and compilers cited in the text.

Author Index

Author Index

Author Index

Author Index

Author Index

Z

TITLE INDEX

This index includes all titles of books, published reports, and theses which are cited in the text. In some cases the titles have been shortened. Journals, titles of articles, and chapter titles are not included.

Title Index

O

SUBJECT INDEX

With the exception of Chicago, Detroit, New York City, and Washington, D.C., individual cities and counties are listed under state name.

A

Academic achievement 12, 49, 52, 179, 184
Advertising firms 27
Aerospace industry 111, 113, 122, 123
Affirmative action 111, 149, 152, 153, 158, 162. See also Equal employment opportunities; Quota employment policies
African identity 41
Agricultural programs 7, 170
Airlines industry 117, 123
American Federation of Labor (AFL) 140
Antitrust laws 145
Apprentice Information Centers 141
Apprenticeship 26, 120, 135, 137, 138, 139, 141
  entrance examination 137, 140
  pretraining 134, 136, 137, 138, 140
  recruitment 140
Armed forces 9, 146, 156, 161
Arrest records 122, 127
Automobile industry 6, 84, 113, 122, 123, 140

B

Banking 27, 81, 84, 87, 88, 113, 117, 129. See also Black capitalism; Capitalism
Barrio 177. See also Ghetto
Becker, Gary 24
Bell Telephone Company 122. See also Utilities industry
Birth rates 60
Black capitalism 81-104. See also Businesses, black-owned; Ghetto, economic development
Blue-collar jobs 20, 126, 127
Boxing, professional 151
Brazil 41
Brimmer, Andrew 87
Brokerage houses 27
Brown v. Board of Education 148
Building trades. See Construction trades; see also Construction industry
Businesses, black-owned 91, 92, 93, 94, 99, 101, 105, 120, 145
  failure of 105
  financing 83
Businesses, Indian-owned 169, 172
Businesses, Mexican-American-owned 182

Subject Index

Subject Index

Subject Index

North, the (cont.)
  school segregation 47, 53
Nutrition 7

O

Occupational attainment 48
Occupational differentials 3, 9, 18,
  75
Occupational distribution 3–29, 100,
  101, 123, 129, 134, 154. See
  also specific field, e.g., Electron-
  ics industry; Managerial positions
Occupational mobility 5, 8, 37
Ohio
  Cleveland 11, 28, 85
Oregon
  Portland 96, 107

P

Paper industry 122, 123
Pennsylvania
  Philadelphia 105, 140, 149, 157
  Pittsburgh 134
Pennsylvania, University of. Wharton
  School of Finance and Commerce
  113, 130
Petroleum industry 113, 119, 123
Police 145
  occupations 147, 154, 161
Political power 6, 27, 89, 94, 96,
  98, 101
Politics 16, 64, 85, 101, 161, 162
Population ix
  analysis 8, 25, 37
  control 98, 172
  explosion 88
  projections 18
Postal Service, U.S. 157
Poverty 6, 11, 17, 100, 147, 155,
  156, 173
  causes 4, 8, 25, 60, 181
  demographic view of 20, 60
  description 26, 177
  effects 13, 25, 39, 178
  solutions 4, 152, 154, 163, 172,
  181
Prejudice 33, 125, 178. See also
  Racism
Private clubs 106

Professional occupations 23
Professional sports 121, 130, 151
Promotion policies 118, 123, 130,
  148
Property tax. See Tax, property
Property values 69, 75
Public housing. See Housing,
  public
Public policies. See Government
  programs
Public utilities. See Utilities in-
  dustry
Public works projects 97
Publishing firms 26
Puerto Ricans 15, 182, 183
  education 51, 185
  employment 13, 27, 59, 74
  housing 74
  medical care 106

Q

Quota employment policies 10,
  135, 145, 146, 150, 153, 157,
  163. See also Equal employment
  opportunities

R

Racism 39, 94, 100, 162. See
  also Prejudice
Railroad industry 123, 126
Real estate industry 74, 76, 78
Recruitment
  apprenticeship 138, 140
  job 8, 62, 116, 118, 120, 147,
  159
Religion 16
Remedial education 47. See also
  Compensatory education
Research methods 38
Reservations, Indian
  control 169
  economic development 170, 172
  education 174
  industrial development 167, 169,
  172, 173
  natural resources 169
Retailing 105–7, 112, 122, 125
Revenue sharing 160